think like a chef

think like a chef

tom colicchio

with catherine young, lori silverbush, and sean fri

photographs by bill bettencourt

clarkson potter/publishers

new york

To the memory of my father, Thomas,
and
for my mother, Beverly

Published by Clarkson Potter/Publishers, New York, New York
Member of the Crown Publishing Group.

Random House, Inc. New York, Toronto, London, Sydney, Auckland
www.randomhouse.com

CLARKSON N. POTTER is a trademark and Potter and colophon
are registered trademarks of Random House, Inc.

Printed in China

Design by Marysarah Quinn

Library of Congress Cataloging-in-Publication Data
Colicchio, Tom.
    Think like a chef / Tom Colicchio with Cathy Young, Lori
Silverbush and Sean Fri; photographs by Bill Bettencourt.—1st ed.
        p. cm.
    1. Cookery.   I. Young, Cathy.   II. Silverbush, Lori.   III. Title.
TX651.C64 2000
641.5—dc21   00-022983

ISBN 0-609-60485-6

10   9   8   7   6   5

contents

foreword by danny meyer

I FIRST ENCOUNTERED TOM COLICCHIO'S FOOD IN 1991, NOT AT his restaurant, Mondrian, but at Share Our Strength's Taste of the Nation—the New York restaurant community's annual charity event to fight hunger. Thirty-six of the city's very best chefs had volunteered to prepare seven hundred tasting portions apiece of their signature dish for a discriminating crowd of foodies. As the event's organizer that year, I learned a lot about the three-dozen chef participants. It's a challenging, hectic night for a chef and the style with which they each approached the evening spoke volumes about them not just as cooks, but also as professionals and human beings. Many were nervous or disorganized, some chose to prepare very simple dishes they knew would be crowd pleasers, and a handful seemed to view the event as a monumental pain in the neck. Then there were the chefs like Tom—who wholeheartedly embraced the anti-hunger mission, and who calmly viewed the event as an opportunity to display his culinary prowess to a group of appreciative gourmets.

Taste of the Nation was a sell-out that evening, keeping me too busy to sample food at many of the chefs' tasting tables. But sensing that I'd be well rewarded, I did make a beeline for Tom Colicchio's table. There I saw a smiling, confident chef plating and serving something that looked odd, yet compelling. Into spiny sea urchin shells he was spooning a fondue of sea urchin, crabmeat, and pureed potatoes, and then sprinkling the rim of each tasting plate with an aromatic curry powder. A few of the less-adventurous guests moved politely along to the next table when they saw what it was. Many others, however, clamored for more. I was salivating. Tom spotted me toward the back of the line and slipped me an urchin when no one was looking.

I can remember the magic perfection of that dish to this day.

Just as it is with winemakers and the wine they produce, you can gauge a lot about the personality of a chef by the style of his food—and vice versa. Watching Tom work that night, and tasting just that one dish, I learned a tremendous amount about him as a chef. Tom is a unique man with a refreshingly personal style of cooking. He cooks like who he is. Tom's food is intelligent and clean; any ingredient on the plate belongs there—period. His dishes have both a tasteful elegance and an un-fussy and uncontrived appearance. His flavor combinations are highly seasonal, of-the-moment ideas that are more instinctive and personal than premeditated and overly intellectualized. He is generous in cooking for your pleasure, not just for his sense of ego. His food is provocative, but it provokes you to think, "Oh yeah, *that* makes sense." A more recent dish of Tom's reminded me of my first taste of that sea urchin dish: Who else could get you to eat Braised Beef Cheeks with Poached Foie Gras and Marrow? You may have never imagined that combination, but knowing Tom, you are confident that he will pull it off, and so you order it and are profoundly happy that you did.

Nearly a decade has passed since I first tasted Tom's food, and were it not for this book, I'd still be wondering how it was conceived. Tom has never been one to talk about why he cooks what he does, and until now the best (and only) way to get inside his chef's mind has been to sit down and eat his food. In *Think Like a Chef,* Tom has opened the door to his culinary process and explained—in straight terms—how his very personal style is actually based on a simple logic that can be employed successfully by anyone who simply loves great food.

Danny Meyer
New York City

preface

I NEVER INTENDED TO WRITE A COOKBOOK. I'VE HAD NUMEROUS requests over the years, but I never wanted to, mostly because for me recipes have never been the point. Frankly, I learned to cook in order to get away from recipes. I couldn't fathom how to capture on the page what inspires me about cooking—the immediacy, the creative process, the integrity of good food. I was often asked to teach classes, and a similar challenge arose there: I couldn't get interested in the mere demonstration of an appetizer, entrée, and dessert, and I was convinced that my students wanted more than that, anyway, based on the questions they asked. Questions like, "Where do you get your ideas?" and "How do you know what goes together?" Instead I hit on the idea of showing how a basic ingredient—roast tomatoes, say, or braised artichokes—can start the chain of creative thought in motion. The class was a hit, and I've been asked to repeat it time and again. Slowly, it got me thinking how to channel the idea—how a chef thinks about food—into a book. The result is in your hand. But in order to fully grasp the concepts I lay out in this book, it might be helpful to understand how I got here in the first place.

My first job, when I was ten, was at the open-air food market in the Italian neighborhood of Elizabeth, New Jersey, where my Uncle George sold vegetables. This was in the days before greenmarkets came into vogue, and we were selling pretty mundane stuff: potatoes and cauliflower, I think. I watched Italian immigrants of my grandparents' generation hovering over each purchase, touching the food, smelling it, picking the perfect chicken to be killed and plucked out back. Each choice was of monumental importance, and it was here that I first became aware of the significance of food in people's lives. These old-timers would never dream of going to a supermarket to buy a plucked, wrapped chicken (no telling what you were getting), and they, in turn, influenced my parents' generation. When I was growing up, we went to Dicosmo's for fresh ricotta and

My grandfather and me, going fishing.

Parmesan, Centanni's pork store for meat (it sold everything, but we called it the pork store), Saracino's for bread. These things were too important to trust to the A&P.

Food, in my house, provided structure to the whole day. On Sundays we would begin, right after ten-o'clock Mass, with a huge egg breakfast. I was one of three growing boys, and we went through a lot of eggs. A few hours later, maybe three or four o'clock, Sunday dinner would begin. There would be cousins, uncles, aunts all over the place. We'd start off with pasta, then meats, salad, and desserts. To a kid, it seemed as though the grown-ups spent the whole day around the table. Just when you'd think they were done, everyone was hungry again and would start in on the leftovers.

My grandfather had a small boat in Barnegat Bay, and I got to go along crabbing and fishing on Saturdays. I'd wake up before dawn to the smell of him frying peppers and onions and eggs—I guess you'd call it a frittata today—which he'd wrap up for us to eat later, on the boat. We would go out on the bay for crabs, to the flats for clams. We brought in everything: weakfish, bluefish, eels—which, skinned and fried, were the most delicious thing you could eat—and when we got home it was my job to clean it all. There was always a big debate on how to boil the crabs—everyone knew of a different recipe—but we always did it the same way: Old Bay seasoning, salt, and boiling water. We'd pull off the shells and the "dead-man's fingers," the gills, and toss the whole crab into a pot of marinara my Grandma Esther had waiting on the stove. Later the crab-flavored sauce would go over linguini, and the crabs would end up in a big bowl in the center of the table. We'd sit with those crabs for hours. Everyone had his or her own method, also a subject of endless debate. This one cleaned all his crabs and saved the meat to the end, that one ate as he went, and so on.

Let me tell you, it was the greatest thing in the world.

Cooking always seemed simple and easy. My parents were both good cooks, but that wasn't considered a remarkable thing. My father liked to re-create restaurant dishes at home, winging it as he went, while my mother preferred to stick with well-loved favorites. I started to cook at about twelve or so, but even then I had no patience for recipes. I would read one and struggle to grasp what it was telling me, then put the recipe away and start. Understanding the whole felt more important than slavishly following each step. I started with my mother's cookbooks, then moved on to a bunch of cookbooks my father brought home from the library at the jail where he worked as a corrections officer. My family became my audience: my brother Mike was an enthusiastic taster from the start and is still my biggest fan. My brother Phil preferred my mother's cooking, and still does. I found a copy of *Cuisine* magazine at my cousin Patty's hair salon and kept it. I remember the issue distinctly; there was an article on Cajun cooking (this was long before Paul Prudhomme was the rage). I made a dish from the issue that sounded good to me, eggplant stuffed with shrimp and Cajun spices. Of course, not having read the recipe through, I didn't realize it was intended as an appetizer. My family liked it fine, but my mother still had to get up and make dinner when we were done.

The summer I was fifteen I got a job in the snack bar at my family's swim club. Don, the short-order cook, and his wife, Lucy, asked me if I wanted to help out for some pocket money. It was never discussed, but before long, Don and I had switched places: I was at the grill, and Don was scooping ice cream. This was great training, because by the time I ended up in fancy restaurants, I was comfortable at a busy stove, using heat, staying on top of many things simultaneously. It was the best summer of my life. I became a quasi-celebrity at the swim club, cooking all day and flirting with girls in just a pair of shorts, no shirt or shoes, long hair trailing down my back. Eventually I got creative and came up with specials—barbecued ribs, grilled sandwiches. Don and Lucy had their best summer ever.

Once school started, I needed a new job. It was a huge event in my neighborhood when Burger King opened up (the sine qua non of teenage employment). The line of kids applying for work went around the block, but I wasted no time on formalities. I marched directly to the manager with my application, as sure of myself as I've ever been. After all, how many fifteen-year-olds had any cooking experience to boast of? I was hired on the spot.

Around this time I was arguing with the nuns and generally bored by school. It was my father who came up with the idea that I might make a good chef. The brochure for the Culinary Institute of America said I needed experience in two restaurants to apply (Burger King didn't count), so I immediately got a job as a prep cook at Evelyn's Seafood Restaurant. Evelyn's started out as a lunch counter in Belmar on the Jersey shore, where Evelyn herself cooked for the construction workers building the bridge over the Shark River Inlet. Over the years it grew into something of an institution, opening a second franchise in Elizabeth. On my first morning, my boss put a tub with sixty pounds of shrimp in front of me and said, "Peel." It felt like hours before I was done, and then he put another sixty pounds in front of me. I could have cried, but I just did what I was told and kept peeling. This went on all day. At ten o'clock that night a waiter poked me in the back, waking me up. I had fallen asleep standing up, over the tub of shrimp.

It was also right around this time that I bought myself a copy of Jacques Pépin's *La Technique*. I guess I realized all along that following recipes couldn't make me into a chef, but learning techniques could. I still remember Pépin's introduction, which I'll paraphrase: Don't read this as if it were a book; treat it as an apprenticeship. I took those words completely to heart. I started to work my way through the book each day after school, starting with chicken stock. With that mastered, the next step, according to Pépin, was to make consommé, which involved creating a protein raft with egg whites to clarify the stock. I did that, too. I tried my hand at pâte à choux: I'd never tasted it in my life, but I had to give it a try. I bought a chicken and some string and trussed it. Then I cut the string off and did it again and again. I bought vegetables to practice my knife skills. For Christmas that year I asked my mother for a Henckels knife, an extravagance at over $100, but there it was, under the tree. I use it to this day.

It started to dawn on me that Evelyn's wasn't exactly a great restaurant, but it was a busy one, and I gradually learned the workings of a bustling enterprise, a valuable lesson. I moved on to pastry where, after turning out 1,200 corn muffins, 20 cheesecakes, and 20 lemon chiffon cakes a day, I discovered I hate to bake. And even though Evelyn's was expanding and trying to standardize its recipes, there was room for creativity. An amazing black man named Slim took me under his wing. Slim was from the South, about sixty years old, and knew everything there was to know about real cooking. He was responsible for the food that required thought and skill: crab-meat stuffing, Thermidor sauce for lobster. Slim had no use for standardized anything and would change the recipes as he saw fit, tasting as he went. I would watch every move he made and ask questions; there was simply nothing he didn't know. I got into the habit of showing up early and making dishes for whoever was around—dishwashers, hostesses—just to experiment. In time I tried my hand at every job in the place, jumping from prep to pastry to line cook. By the time I left Evelyn's I was responsible for all the purchasing and receiving, a skill that serves me well to this day.

I went next to an Italian restaurant, a job that lacked distinction in all ways but one: I left knowing how to butcher. Sirloins, tenderloins, poultry, you name it. Learning to butcher an entire leg of veal—an intimidating hunk of meat if ever there was one—gave me a new sense of confidence. Years later, at the Quilted Giraffe, there was a day when whole baby lambs came through the door. The other cooks just stared at them. I dove in and butchered one after the other while everyone watched in silence. Well, we couldn't exactly serve them whole, could we?

I left the Italian restaurant and took a job at a restaurant that had just opened. I expected The Old Mansion would be an upscale place, since it was on the grounds of a country club in a beautiful turn-of-the-century home. Two Culinary Institute alumni were hired to run the kitchen. At this point, I was nineteen and still considering attending CIA, so I looked forward to working with two recent graduates. They were mostly doing renditions of classics, which was fine, but I knew from my reading of food magazines that there was more out there than Chicken Cordon Bleu and Steak Diane. It was time to move on.

I took a job as a hotel cook in Secaucus, New Jersey. I was the youngest person in the kitchen, which was a little intimidating, but after a week they promoted me to dinner chef. Suddenly it was my job to create menus and specials for their dining room, and it was here that I began to realize my limitations. I would read books by Frédy Girardet, Michel Guérard, and Alain Chapel, and I could see (even if no one else could) that my dishes were missing the mark. It wasn't just about techniques, after all; there was something intangible I hadn't picked up. I realized I had to find a job someplace where I could learn more.

Around this time, a movement known as Nouvelle Cuisine was in vogue, and from that had sprung the idea of a new style of American food. Chefs like Larry Forgione and Wolfgang Puck were gaining the limelight; *Cuisine* magazine ran a piece on California cooking, which I studied. Food suddenly had become big, and the chefs—with their individual styles and personalities—were news. I saw an ad for a new restaurant in Millburn, New Jersey, seeking someone to help cook "the New American Cuisine." That got my attention. My girlfriend and I went in to 40 Main Street for dinner, to see it for ourselves. The food was different from anything I'd tasted—creative, exciting. The menu was small and emphasized fresh ingredients. I applied the next day and got the job.

Working at 40 Main Street was a great experience. There was no fixed menu; we'd simply show up every day and see which ingredients were great. Whatever we chose formed the basis for that night's menu. The chef and sous-chef sought my input and my mind stretched around the ideas, playing and experimenting with ingredients. We began to appear in local papers. We received three stars in the *New York Times* and suddenly we were packed every night, which created a new set of demands and taught me how to deal with that. For the first time I gained an understanding of the role the media played in the entire equation. It felt like we had hit the big time, and in a way we had. Even so, I had never ventured from my home turf of New Jersey, and soon the sous-chef Jerry Bryan, who had worked at the Bridge Café with Leslie Revsin, was urging me to give New York a try.

In the dim, outer regions of my provincial mind, I was aware of the great New York restaurants: La Côte Basque, Lutèce, La Réserve. But now there were new places, like Quilted Giraffe, Jams, and a fledgling up-and-comer called Gotham Bar and Grill, that were doing the kinds of things we did at 40 Main Street. Like many people before me, I was sure that a job in New York would be my one and only shot at the big time, not to be attempted until I was at the top of my game. Also, in my circle of friends, New York was somewhere you went for a night of running around, doing unprintable things before heading back to Elizabeth, where real life happened. The idea of driving into the city every day was as alien as commuting to Appalachia. Still, at Jerry's urging, I decided to give it a shot.

I shopped my résumé around, and Alfred Portale, who was at Gotham Bar and Grill for all of a week, hired me. Gotham was on the verge of closing because the original concept—a fusion Moroccan thing—hadn't taken hold. Alfred had been brought in to turn the place around, and I guess he thought I might be helpful. A week into it, however, I got a call from Barry Wine, owner of the Quilted Giraffe, offering me a job. Alfred, being a nice guy, understood my defection. At the time Quilted Giraffe was *the* place to go: a four-star restaurant with astronomical prices and—the best part—a reasonable, five-day workweek. Most important, they were doing more exciting things on the plate than I'd ever seen.

It wasn't my New Jersey résumé that got me hired. The Quilted Giraffe was on the verge of expanding. Barry knew that to do so he would have to go to a six-day week (like everyone else) and hire what he called "career cooks." Prior to this he preferred a sort of kitchen counterculture, filling the place with writers, artists, and people in the midst of a career change, all of whom had no preconceived notions of how things "should" be done in a kitchen. Barry, himself a former lawyer, had devised an unconventional split-second method of line cooking—completely unique—and it worked well. Barry needed a lab rat (me), to see if a career cook would fit into this environment. I guess he decided I did, since four months later he made me sous-chef.

All restaurants start off the night, before the guests arrive, with "family meal." At family, the staff eats, tastes new dishes, and discusses the upcoming service. One night at family Barry mentioned that, as a favor to one of his line cooks, he would be allowing her fiancé—an aspiring chef—and his friend into the kitchen to observe us in action. Both visitors were Midwesterners, intent on opening a restaurant in New York. Danny Meyer walked through the door, looking too young to shave. I remember thinking, from my hotshot vantage of twenty-two, that here was a guy who was going to get eaten alive in New York. He watched respectfully from the sidelines as we did our work—plating Barry's signature beggars' purses in swift six-second intervals. To his untrained eye, it must have been baffling, but I guess he took something from the experience because he turned around and opened Union Square Cafe.

Soon after, I got a call from Dan Cannizio, the owner of 40 Main Street, who needed help. The chef had left abruptly, despite being scheduled to teach a cooking class on pasta to a sold-out audience the following week. I went out and winged it, and Dan suggested that I stay on as executive chef. I welcomed the chance to improve away from the lights of New York and agreed on the condition that my old friend Jerry Bryan come on board as co-chef. Dan agreed, and I was back in New Jersey. Running a kitchen with Jerry was a great experience, both for what I learned and for the relationships I formed: It was there I met John Schaeffer, who came to 40 Main Street as an extern. Years later he worked for me at Mondrian and later became my right hand as chef de cuisine at Gramercy Tavern. Despite it all, I still felt that I was missing something. I asked my friend Ariane Daguin to arrange a *stage*—a learn-while-you-work stint—at her father's highly regarded inn and restaurant, l'Hôtel d'France, in Gascony.

The first thing that struck me when I got to Gascony was the rustic, beautiful countryside, unlike anything I'd ever seen. Gascony is the duck, foie gras, and wild game capital of France, and the local restaurants place an emphasis on hearty cooking—cassoulets, and the like. I was to live upstairs and work in the kitchens, all the while learning the routine of a Michelin two-star establishment. It was a great setup for a young cook, except for the days the inn was overbooked and I had to haul all my things to a crummy boardinghouse nearby. Although I didn't speak a word of French, the cooks taught me by doing, so the language barrier wasn't a big deal (it *was* an issue when I tried to meet girls, but that's another story). On a typical day, I would roll out of bed at dawn, grab a croissant and a cup of coffee, and work all morning. I'd head upstairs midafternoon for a shower and a nap (*repose,* in French), read the *Herald Tribune* in a neighborhood café for an hour or so, and return to the restaurant at around four o'clock. I'd work like a dog until after ten, then head to the pub for drinks and sign language with the locals for a few hours until I fell into bed. The next day I'd wake up and do it again. About two months into my *stage,* another American showed up. Kerry Heffernan, thankfully, had more working French than I, and knew his way around a kitchen. Today he is the chef at Eleven Madison Park, and we are still fast friends and fishing partners.

One morning I stumbled out of bed, hungover as usual, and went down to the kitchen. As I sipped my coffee, I groggily became aware of a massive box—at least three feet long and almost as wide. From one end, a pair of long, floppy ears extended, dragging on the floor. At the other end poked a pair of hairy, padded feet. It dawned on me that Bugs's ugly wild cousin was lying in a box, waiting to be butchered. The French cooks, looking for a laugh, decided to let the dumb American have a go at it. I dimly remembered, from my days of studying Jacques Pépin's book, the section on skinning a rabbit. How much harder could wild hare be? I grabbed a knife and laid into the gigantic, hairy beast. I gained respect that day from my French coworkers, but it was a grisly morning.

The best thing about my *stage* at l'Hotel de France was the food that came through the doors each day. Ortolans—the tiny bite-size birds intended to be eaten whole—and *allouettes,* even smaller, which we would roast on a skewer with a cèpe and a piece of goose liver. Huge unblemished whole foie gras of a quality I've never seen since. Wild ducks, pheasant, and *polomba* (wild pigeons). At the restaurants I'd worked at in the States, poultry came plucked and ready to go, but in France everything arrived in full plumage. A pair of tough old Portuguese washerwomen were in charge of plucking, and I learned early to stay out of their way. After they were finished with the larger feathers, the tiny pinfeathers had to be singed off over a flame—a nasty, smelly job that, naturally, fell to me.

Every day a man showed up in a truck piled with fresh vegetables picked from local farms, and the cooks would go out back to choose what we needed. I learned by watching the customers and townspeople with their amazing respect for food. I suspect this was a legacy of the postwar years, when food was scarce. The way the food was cultivated and handled, its treatment in the kitchen, was a revelation to me. I also learned a lesson about ingredients. Far better to offer a few dishes made of the freshest, most immediate ingredients than a menu filled with everything under the sun, made from mediocre food. It was here that I learned that even the most elegant food should be derived from good, honest ingredients.

When I returned from France I heard of a new restaurant, Rakel, that was looking for cooks. The chef was Thomas Keller, a tall, intense man who hired me as a cook but promoted me to sous-chef soon after. Working with Thomas was a great experience. Each morning we would look over the food that had arrived that day and talk about what we could do with it, how far we could take the ingredients, while retaining their essence. It was an exciting, creative time. There were nights when I would work the fish side of the line, while Thomas worked meat, the ideas flying back and forth between us. Guests would show up for tasting dinners and have no idea what they were getting, which only made sense since we had no idea either until we started to cook.

Thomas was a slave driver, but also a generous collaborator. I was encouraged to come up with new dishes in the middle of service. Run with it. There was a willingness at Rakel to move away from conventions, to see where our imaginations and techniques could take us. It was here that I first saw food placed right up on the outer rim of the plate—something that shook up my ideas of presentation. Once, for a large party, we took an entire lobe of foie gras and roasted it like a chicken, just to see what would happen. There were things we would (thankfully) never do again—like splatter effects created by dripping beet juice from two feet above the plate—but I soaked it all in. I came to see that to distinguish yourself as a chef, you had to take all the training and experiences you had gained and use them in pursuit of one thing only: your own distinct style. All the chefs I admired were doing exactly this. At Gotham, Alfred Portale was emerging as a pioneer of height on the plate; at Rakel, Thomas was using ingredients in a way that was focused but experimental and unique. Developing my own style was my next challenge.

When my old friend Jerry called from Virginia in the fall of 1988, I went down to help him open a new restaurant. I worked with Jerry for about nine months, enjoying the weather and the warmth of Jerry's family, who treated me like another son. Still, I missed the energy and pulse of the big city. On a visit home I ran into Dennis Foy, the chef and an owner of Mondrian, a new restaurant in Midtown, who offered me a job. I was at Mondrian for only a couple weeks when my father was diagnosed with late-stage lung cancer. I took a leave of absence to be with him and my family. My father, for whom I'm named, died just around the holidays, a sad time. A little while later, I returned to the kitchen at Mondrian as chef de cuisine, planning the menu and overseeing the day-to-day activities of the kitchen.

I read an article in the *New York Times* magazine by Paula Wolfert about Michel Bras, a rising chef in France. Bras was known for going on foraging excursions into the hills surrounding the Massif Central mountains, looking for wild ingredients. I was intrigued and wanted to see this for myself, so I arranged for a *stage* at his eponymous two-star restaurant in the town of Lagouile.

Michel opened my eyes to a new, natural approach to food. In addition to using the wild greens he found out and about, he was one of the first chefs I ever saw to experiment with herbed oils as an alternative to more traditional sauces. Michel believed in cooking things slowly, without searing or roasting. He was famous for preparing salmon in a very low oven, with a tray of water down below. Over time this would steam the fish, imparting a wonderful, ethereal texture. Michel was also the first to make a dessert that is now ubiquitous on New York menus: the molten chocolate cake. I loved it so much, I borrowed it for my own menu—the only time I've ever copied someone else's food.

I would have stayed longer at Michel Bras but Robert Scott, the principal owner of Mondrian, called and asked me to come back early. Dennis Foy was having second thoughts about running a restaurant in New York and was anxious to return to New Jersey. I came on as executive chef, just as the greenmarket movement was beginning in the States. Suddenly I was able to find the kind of ingredients that were rarely seen on restaurant menus at the time, like ramps, borage, chickweed, and purslane, and I could put into practice the things I'd learned in Lagouile. I contacted a man in Washington State who sent me incredible wild hyssop, mountain sorrel, and amaranth. I started to source out seeds for unusual ingredients, which I would give to local farmers to grow for Mondrian. At the same time, food began to appear in the Union Square Greenmarket that made cooking a new adventure, and the relationship between chefs and farmers became symbiotic: The better the quality, the more the chefs bought. The more the chefs bought, the harder the farmers worked to cultivate new (or old and forgotten) produce.

With ingredients like that at my disposal, I worked further at Mondrian to develop a language of cooking that was my own. Serious "foodies"—those New Yorkers who follow chefs and know everything that's happening in the restaurant world—started to show up. Often they asked to meet me, so I learned to keep a clean apron by the kitchen door and to act civilized. Eight months after Dennis left, on October 12, 1990, I got my first three-star review in the *New York Times*. When *Food & Wine* published a list of the ten best new chefs of 1990, I was on it. Chefs I had long admired—Jean-Jacques Racheau, Jonathan Waxman, Daniel Boulud—came in to see what I was doing. It was a heady time. I was twenty-seven years old.

Mondrian's owners had signed a lease for our Fifty-ninth Street space in the late eighties, when the real estate market was at an all-time high. After the stock market crashed, that deal coupled with a cringing economy meant the restaurant—even though we were busy—wasn't making money. Despite the good reviews, I wasn't happy working this hard and losing money every month. I asked the owners to close the restaurant, while I searched for a more favorable rent deal in a different neighborhood.

Over the years Danny Meyer had been a frequent diner at Mondrian with his wife, Audrey. It seemed to me, as I looked around for a new location, that partnering with a talented restaurateur— someone who could concentrate on the front of the house, while I focused on the food—would be a good way to go. Danny had earned a reputation for great service at Union Square Cafe and was well loved in the restaurant community. He was a vocal proponent of a new type of service in fine restaurants: friendly, knowledgeable, and unpretentious. This felt like a good fit for the type of food I wanted to do—intense, but honest and unaffected. I had spent some time with Danny at the *Food & Wine* festival in Aspen, and I got the feeling that he might be looking to branch out beyond Union Square Cafe. Months later I called him to tell him I was closing down Mondrian. I suggested we put our heads together on a new place.

We sat down in Union Square Park to talk it over, and discovered we held a lot of the same ideas about the kind of business we wanted to run. We talked about our families, what we valued, and what we felt was missing in the restaurant world. We talked about creating an American restaurant that had the finest food and perfect service, without sacrificing warmth. Today, the concept is widespread, but back then it was a brand-new idea. We decided to take a trip to Italy, just the two of us, to see how we got along. Danny and I traveled together for ten days, eating our way through Piedmont and Tuscany. On the flight home, we sketched out a plan for Gramercy Tavern.

I'm about as lucky as a chef/restaurateur can be at Gramercy Tavern. The restaurant continues to attract the most talented, dedicated staff I've ever come across, like Claudia Fleming, whose desserts have made her a food celebrity in her own right. Like cooks who spend long hours on their feet, patiently and skillfully making my ideas happen. Like waitstaff that leave diners with a lasting impression of intelligence and kindness. They all make me look good. And when I hear—as I often do—that one of my former cooks has gone on to become chef or pastry chef in another restaurant, I feel as proud as any parent.

My relationships with farmers like Guy Jones, Rick Bishop, and Tim Eckertson have been an important part of getting where we are today. When veal or chicken has been raised in a clean environment, as it is on Steve and Sylvia Pryzant's farm in Pennsylvania, carefully hand-fed organic grain and allowed to grow, uncrowded, with good air and gentle handling, it becomes something tremendous on the plate. The less you do to it—or to the perfect mushroom, or that ripe, heirloom tomato—the more you can appreciate its exceptional quality. Over the last few years, my cooking has evolved to showcase this—most recently at my new restaurant, Craft. Respect for great ingredients permeates my cooking and is an important part of the thought process of being a chef.

Ironically, the older I get, the simpler my tastes become. Looking at pictures of my food at Mondrian, I see how much fancier I was

The Gramercy Tavern crowd. They all make me look good.

then. These days I'm excited by purity. I've started searching for the absolute essence of ingredients, veering away from showmanship and toward food that is clean and elemental. The cooks in my kitchen know just how hard it is to cook something perfectly—it requires intense focus and split-second timing. When there is little on the plate to obscure the food, mistakes of execution and quality have nowhere to hide. It has to be exact, perfect, true. This is truly a challenge for a chef, one that keeps me interested as I cook day after day for the most demanding diners on the planet.

I love my job, so in the end it feels great to have set down on paper what I love best about cooking, namely the visceral thrill of transforming great ingredients—tasting, listening, and touching as I go—into soulful, uncluttered food. What you hold in your hand is not a book of fancy restaurant recipes, nor is it an attempt to "translate" my ideas for the home cook. It is simply a book about what I find exciting about cooking, and the creative process—"thinking like a chef"—that gets me there.

introduction

EVERY SO OFTEN I'M ASKED TO TEACH COOKING CLASSES. As I lay out my ingredients and start to talk I notice the same thing happening over and over again. Out come the notebooks and pens, and down go the heads. I begin speaking and the students start scribbling. They jot down everything that comes out of my mouth word for word, ingredient for ingredient, step for step. Soon, the questions start:

"What brand do you use?"—I tell them.
"Can you repeat that?"—I usually do.
"How long do you cook that?"—My standard reply: "Till it's done."

This last one usually meets with a few weak smiles and a slightly hostile silence. Till it's done? How am I going to know when it's done, if he doesn't tell me? Usually at around this point I ask that everyone put the notebooks down. Just watch and listen, I urge, and you will learn much more about how I cook than you will if you try to write down every word I say. Then I pass out copies of the recipes (so they will have them) and explain that cooking is a craft best learned through observation and practice. Leave the class with an understanding of *how* to cook and I will be much happier than if you leave with a copy of my lecture. In fact, I say, if I do my job right, they'll be able to take that knowledge home with them and alter the recipe to their own personal tastes.

This is also usually met with silence. Alter your recipe? Why in the world would we want to do that? Simple. As the seasons change, so will the variety and quality of ingredients available. And maybe you hate peas but love asparagus. The technique remains the same, so *of course* you're going to want to alter the recipe! After a few nervous titters, my audience can usually be persuaded to leave off the pen and paper and start watching as I work with the food, play with it, create a few basic building blocks based on simple ingredients, and take off from there. At the end of the class, students usually approach me, the proverbial lightbulbs glowing over their heads, and say something like, "Now I get it!" This always brings to mind the time I finally convinced my seven-year-old, Dante, to jump off a diving board: He inched his way to the end of the board, mistrust written all over his face, and then finally—against his better judgment—jumped. In moments he surfaced, sputtering and shouting, "Again!" I'd like all my students to want to rush home and do it again.

so which comes first— the chef or the recipe?

Probably the number one question I'm asked on any given day is "How do you come up with your recipes?" The truth is, I *don't*. I don't sit down and "create" food combinations. In fact, the majority of food combinations "create" themselves. And I sure don't start sitting down. I start in the marketplace, walking. On any given day, I'll walk through the Union Square Greenmarket (although any well-stocked supermarket will do) and see what looks good. What's abundant? What's growing together naturally? Which herbs are peaking? Above all, what are the seasons saying? For me, and I would guess most chefs, *creating begins in the marketplace*. What I see starts me thinking about flavors and textures, combinations and balance. Then I bring my purchases home and set to work applying the techniques I've learned over the years. *Voilà!* A recipe. Which leads me to:

the best meal ever

Another question I'm frequently asked is "Where do you like to eat?" The implication is that as a chef I have the inside track on where to go, or at least can distinguish truly good food from everything else out there. I'm embarrassed to admit that I don't get out much. Without exception, the greatest meals of my life have taken place at home. And not necessarily my home. Okay, you're thinking. That's not fair. You're a chef. Of course your home meals are great (not necessarily, but that's another story). And your friends are probably chefs, too (most aren't, but that's also beside the point). The Best Meal Ever happened at a friend's farmhouse in Maryland one early fall afternoon, the kind of day that still looks and feels like summer but with an unmistakable hint of the crisp green-apple autumn that lies ahead. With the Redskins season opener in the background and a batch of icy mint juleps urging us along, a group of friends—an MBA and a musician, a couple of doctors, a salesperson (in other words *non-chefs*), and I—waltzed out to the backyard garden and plucked everything and anything that looked ripe and ready to go. No one, save myself, had any professional cooking experience, and we sure didn't set out with a specific meal plan or recipe in mind. Like the conductor of an amateur orchestra, I set different people to different tasks without inquiring first, "Do you know how to sauté an onion?" If they didn't, they just asked and I showed them, and on we went. No one had any idea where we were headed (myself included), but we were hungry and liked good food, so we just let the ingredients dictate which path to take. And to this day the meal of baked polenta layered with fresh vegetables and the sirloin with roasted peppers and sweet onions figures as one of the best of my life. Impromptu. Delicious.

so what's my point?

The point is that I intend to teach you to think a little like I do, so that you can make The Best Meal Ever whenever you want to. This is what I do in my classes and this is what I hope to do here. How? By sharing my techniques and knowledge of ingredients but more important, by sharing my passion and approach to food. My ultimate goal is to free you from the feeling that you *must* follow a recipe—to help you trust your instincts and let fresh, seasonal ingredients dictate the way to go. I hope that you'll leave this book with the confidence to walk through the greenmarket, or grocery, or neighborhood bodega without a recipe, open to what you find there, but with the ability—using basic, time-honored techniques—to put those ingredients together skillfully and intelligently.

a word about techniques

Cooking is a craft that begins with technique. Learning these techniques is a bit like learning a new language. If you've ever learned a foreign language, you know there's a point when you stop translating each word in your head, and can understand—first phrases, then sentences, and finally, the entire gist of the thing. Part of the process is learning the shorthand that is common to speakers of the same language and practically meaningless to everyone else.

You see this everywhere: Ever hear doctors talk among themselves? Or physicists? Wine people use terms like "watery meniscus" that mean nothing to a layperson. When giving instructions to a sous-chef, I use chef language, ". . . braise the fish in a little beurre fondue, sweat some peas, ramps, and morels . . ." I trust that he or she will know how to make a beurre fondue, knows what I mean by braise, and will instinctively grasp the correct ratios of fish to peas.

Of course, everything changes when a guest comes to my restaurant and asks, "How do I make this at home?" Suddenly I need to leave the kitchen patois behind and break it down. How do I choose fresh fish? How do I fillet it and season it? How do I make beurre fondue? Will that be the sauce for the finished dish? How do I cook the peas? The morels? And what the heck are ramps, anyway? What if I can't find these ingredients? How do I know this all goes together? And what do I mean by "braise"? Or "blanch"? Or "roast," for that matter? In this book, I answer these questions, starting with the basic techniques. And although I will walk you through each recipe, my goal is to have you—the lay cook with a passion for food—learn some of the chef shorthand for yourself. Then you can take these steps—building blocks to great recipes—work them into your own repertoire, and apply them to the ingredients you like best.

My goal is to have you learn some chef shorthand for yourself.

how to use the book

This book is organized in a way designed to get you thinking as I do—to look first and foremost at ingredients in terms of basic **Techniques:** roasting, braising, blanching, sweating, stock-making, and sauce-making. Get these down, and you've mastered the most fundamental tools to creating great recipes.

Next the book focuses on the creative process of a chef and on "ingredients." Why the quotes? Because I'm not referring to singular items, necessarily. When I walk through the greenmarket, I don't see piles of raw vegetables like the next guy. I see them through a chef lens, some as star soloists, others combined in tried and untried directions. Braised, roasted, or sweated, together or alone, these make up the "ingredients" that inspire recipes.

I've tried to illustrate this idea with a chapter I call **Studies.** Each of the studies highlights one ingredient as a basic building block—for example, roasted tomatoes—that can be utilized in simple or complex ways, depending on your needs, your time limit, or your ambition. Do you want to dazzle guests or feed a hungry kid? My hope is that this chapter will get you thinking outward, from one ingredient to many dishes. Then comes a chapter I call **Trilogies,** which provides recipes centered around three ingredients that marry well—for example, duck, root vegetables, and apples. Using a variety of techniques, the same three ingredients can yield any number of combinations and possibilities for a great meal. The only limits are time and inclination.

Next is a chapter on **Component Cooking**, the method by which I mix and match ingredients on the plate. To illustrate the way I think about components, I've focused mostly on vegetables, broken down by season, with recipes and suggested combinations. And I conclude with a short section about some **Favorites**, like foie gras and oysters (see pages 251 to 255). Follow these suggestions to the letter and you can re-create the dishes I serve in my restaurants and at home. However, if you come across a combination you love—except for, say, the braised red cabbage—then go ahead and substitute mashed potatoes. Nothing is sacred or written in stone. I will forgive you. In fact, I'll be thrilled. Because when you do, you'll be thinking like a chef.

I urge you to read all the way through sections of this book—even parts you may think don't apply to you because they seem complicated or time consuming. If you can, follow the progression I've set out for you here, from techniques to ingredients, from one idea to many, since I truly feel it will give you insight into my creative process. You'll see, as I have, that a basic love of great ingredients and an open mind are all you really need to think like a chef.

Do you want to dazzle guests or feed a hungry kid?

techniques

roasting

m<small>Y PARTNER AT</small> G<small>RAMERCY</small> T<small>AVERN,</small> D<small>ANNY</small> M<small>EYER,</small> likes to say that the best way to get people to try something new is to let them know it is roasted. The term manages to conjure comfort food and adventurous cooking simultaneously, along with an image of gorgeously browned edges and caramelized flavor. Lamb, beef, pork, venison, rabbit, squab, chicken and turkey, foie gras, whole fish, fish fillets, lobster, almost every vegetable: you name it, I roast it.

Roasting, simply put, is cooking with dry heat, traditionally over or in front of an open flame. Most often, the word "roast" implies oven cooking, but I use the word as shorthand for both oven roasting and pan roasting. They are both the exact same technique, but oven roasting, as the name implies, involves transferring the pan to a hot oven to complete the process. Pan roasting finishes the food in the same pan, on top of the stove.

As a rule, I prefer pan roasting. It allows me to effect a transformation on something almost immediately. Roasting in an oven cheats me of the audible, visual, and tactile cues that are such a gratifying step of the cooking process. For some people, the end result alone— the perfectly browned sea bass, the crisp chicken—is the point, but for me the process of browning the meat, watching the sugars in the surface caramelize, and listening to the sizzling sound of the butter, the sputter as the moisture in the herbs meets the juices in the pan, is as satisfying as the result. Watching as the dish transforms from a group of separate, inert ingredients into a new thing altogether is rewarding even before the first bite. When you learn to pan roast for yourself, a practical benefit is that in time you'll come to recognize the audible and visual cues of correctly cooked food, and you'll find yourself relying less and less on the times and temperatures printed in any recipe.

If I had all day I imagine I'd even cook larger roasts this way. But I don't, and neither do you. Transferring a large piece of meat or fish to the oven allows you to complete the process without standing for hours next to the stove, turning the food. That is not to say that you can transfer a roast to the oven and forget about it. You can't. Even in the oven, the surface that is in contact with the hot pan will roast more quickly than the rest, and the food still needs to be basted. But, loosely speaking, oven roasting allows you to free up the stovetop and yourself (somewhat) to work on something else.

basic roasting technique
These steps apply to pan roasting and oven roasting alike.

1. Brown the food on top of the stove, in a pan with a small amount of oil, at about medium heat. Browning helps to get the cooking started, moves the juices toward the center of the roast, and ensures a nicely cooked exterior. Don't worry about the food sticking to the pan during this step. If you pat it completely dry first, use only medium or medium-high heat, and be patient, the food will release itself from the pan when it's browned. You'll know when you've attained the correct heat by the "sound" of the pan: The oil should sizzle, but not pop and sputter, as the food cooks.

2. Avoid using high heat, both on the stove and in the oven (temperatures of 325° F. to 375° F. usually work best). Although it is tempting to roast at a high heat, you'll get the best results in terms of flavor and texture by treating the ingredients gently. Contrary to what many recipes say, you do not need to start the oven at a higher temperature, then lower it halfway through.

3. Add some butter to the pan about three-quarters of the way through cooking. It will melt quickly and commingle with the juices from the roast, creating a liquid for basting. This is usually when I add some herbs to the pan. **Baste** the roast with the liquids in the pan.

4. Let the food rest. The juices will have been forced to the center by the heat. During the resting period they will have a chance to redistribute

Baste the roast to keep the outside fibers from drying out. No fancy equipment needed— a spoon, filled from the pan and tipped over the food, works just fine.

If your roast is relatively fatty, like most poultry, begin basting as soon as you see fat and juices in the bottom of the pan. Adding butter too early could cause it to burn.

themselves. If you've properly basted the roast, the outer flesh will have no problem reabsorbing these juices. You can omit this step for fish and vegetables.

It only seems complicated on the page. In practice it is anything but. Just keep repeating to yourself: **Brown, gently roast, baste, rest.** This same technique works equally well for foods we don't explicitly cover in this chapter—like venison or pork. The only thing that differs is length of time the food cooks until done. Fish obviously takes less time, as do thinner cuts or single portions of meat. Aha! you're thinking. That's why I need a recipe. To know when it's done! But actually, there are a number of ways to test for doneness. You might find it easiest to use a meat thermometer to see if you've achieved the temperature you like (see the box on page 34) or you can pierce it with a knife and see if the juices run clear. A trick I especially like for large cuts of meat is to stick a long metal skewer completely through the roast, leave it there for a moment, then pull it out and press it against my upper lip. If it feels warmer than my skin, I know that the center of the roast is approaching medium rare (125°F.).

If you do rely on a meat thermometer, make a habit of pressing the meat or fish with your finger once it's done and noticing the resistance you feel. If you like your food rare, there should be plenty of "give" to the flesh. At medium, you will be able to press down, but there will be some underlying firmness as well. At well done, the meat will be quite firm, without much give at all. Try to remember the feel of food cooked the way you like it. Eventually you will be able to rely on this tactile method, and you may be able to do away with the thermometer altogether.

Vegetables are cooked through when they are pierced easily with the tip of a knife. Guidelines for fish are hard to give here, since people vary widely on how they like their fish cooked. Usually, when fish turns opaque, it is cooked through. (I like it when it still has a touch of translucence, except in the case of very meaty fish, such as tuna, which I like seared on the edges and rare in the center.) Try to take fish out of the pan a few moments before it's done, as it will continue to cook on its own.

The recipes that follow have suggested cooking times. Please remember, a recipe can't take into account variables like size and

If you'd like to check your temperatures with a meat thermometer until you've mastered a feel for when things are done, the following are approximate guidelines. Keep checking during cooking, and try to remove the roast just before it achieves the desired texture or temperature, as it will continue to cook for a minute or so out of the oven or pan.

red meats	120°F.—rare (red cool center)
	125°F.—medium rare (red warm center)
	130°F.—medium (pink center)
	135°F.—medium well (small pink center)
	140°F.—well done (no pink)
pork or veal	140°F.—medium
	150°F.—well done
poultry	160°F.—white meat cooked
	170°F.—dark meat cooked
fish*	120°F.—medium rare
	130°F.—medium/cooked through

*Cooking temperatures (and hence times) for fish vary too widely to chart with absolute certainty. Go by firmness, flakiness (you can test with a thin-blade knife), and color. Check early and often.

thickness of the food, or variations in oven temperature. Even if you can control your oven's temperature with an oven thermometer, a recipe's cooking time should serve as a general guideline only. Check the food earlier than the recipe states and keep checking until it's done.

sweating

As an alternative to pan roasting, I occasionally call for vegetables to be **sweated** in a small pan on the stove. Sweating is much more gentle than roasting. To sweat, as we say in "chefspeak," means to cook without color. This is accomplished by cooking the vegetables gently in a small amount of butter or oil, until they are cooked through. As they cook, the vegetables will "sweat" or release some liquid. Again, you start with a pan heated to medium, and add the vegetables slowly. They should sizzle, but only slightly, and give off a little steam. You should move the vegetables around a bit, unlike in pan roasting, to keep them from caramelizing.

Sweating is basic to many stocks and sauces. Sweated vegetables are also important in dishes like ratatouille or onion relish, in which you require a more neutral onion flavor, not the pronounced caramelized flavor that results from browning.

a word about sautéing

Sautéing is a technique of cooking small pieces of food quickly, in a small amount of oil or butter, while moving them rapidly in a shallow pan. I rarely use this method because, as a rule, I like to cook food whole, preferring the deeper flavors that result from a longer cooking time. Sautéing is useful, however, if you want to cook small pieces of fish or bay scallops.

The word "sauté" comes from the French verb to jump; the small pieces of food literally jump in the pan, due to the heat from a high flame. (You'll soon see how I feel about cooking things at a very high heat.) Unlike sweating, sautéing does allow the food to brown. When sautéing, the oil should be hot enough so that the food doesn't stick, but not so hot that the oil is smoking. Make sure to pat the food dry; if it's wet it will create steam, which will inhibit browning. Do not crowd the pan, since this will also create unwanted steam. It's better to sauté in batches if you are cooking a large amount.

high heat is not your friend

Although it may be tempting to use a high heat when you roast, DON'T. One skill that I think separates accomplished cooks from all the rest is their ability to control heat. How do you do that? You watch, *listen,* smell, and check frequently. There is not some mystical-chef-intuitive-thing happening here. The cues are simple and evident to anyone once you know what to look for. I particularly find myself listening to the pan: A nice, low sizzle is about right. If the sizzle is very loud, it means the pan is too hot, so I lower the heat. If I can't hear anything, I raise it. As foods cook, they become more aromatic. If the heat is too high, that smell becomes charred as the sugars in the food caramelize, then burn. Turn on your senses and don't be afraid to adjust the heat as you go.

Just as you wouldn't put food into a cold oven while it comes up to temperature, don't put food into a cold pan. You should always heat the pan to a medium heat before adding the food. As it heats, oil should slide easily in the pan. The food will lower the temperature of the pan slightly. As the food cooks and the pan gets hotter, you should lower the temperature slightly to compensate. The goal is to maintain a consistently medium temperature. How do you know if the pan is at the right heat to start the food? With vegetables, one trick is to throw one (or a small piece of one) in and see what happens. If you get a good, low sizzle and it starts to cook, you're there. If it doesn't do much at all, then you need to wait for the pan to reach the right heat. If the vegetable sizzles loudly and quickly starts to burn, you need to lower the heat.

If you are roasting vegetables, it is very important not to throw all the vegetables into the pan at once (I call it crowding the pan). Most vegetables have a high water content, and if they are crowded they'll start to steam instead of roast. Instead, add them to the pan in small amounts, watching and listening to make sure the pan stays at a consistent temperature. Continue adding at intervals until they are all in the pan.

This also applies to liquids: When you add liquid, do it slowly to maintain the temperature of the whole. I think of this the way I do the air-conditioning at Gramercy Tavern; we start off the night at a reasonable temperature, but as more people enter the room, we have to constantly adjust the thermostat to maintain the right level. Don't be afraid to raise and lower the heat as you go.

All of my recipes call for kosher salt instead of table salt. Kosher salt is more porous, and therefore less salty than table salt; using it allows me to evenly salt the entire length of the food without it becoming too salty. I also use unsalted butter as I cook, so that I can control the saltiness of the recipe myself—first, when I season the uncooked roast, and last, when I finish it with a light sprinkling of coarse sea salt, which has a nice, clean (unchemical) flavor. (For more on salt, see page 125.)

roasted chicken

See the photograph on page 30.

1 (3- to 3½-pound) free-range chicken
    (see sidenote)
Kosher salt and freshly ground black
    pepper
2 sprigs of fresh rosemary

2 sprigs of fresh thyme
1 tablespoon peanut oil
2 tablespoons unsalted butter
Coarse sea salt

1. Heat the oven to 375°F. Rinse the chicken and dry thoroughly with paper towels. Cut off the last joint of the wing and discard. Season the chicken liberally inside and out with kosher salt and pepper, place the rosemary and thyme inside the cavity, then truss.

2. Heat the oil in a large, heavy ovenproof skillet over medium heat until it moves easily across the pan. Place the chicken on its side in the skillet and brown, about 7 minutes. Turn and brown the other side, about 7 minutes more. Place the chicken breast-side up and transfer the skillet to the oven. Roast for about 20 minutes, then add butter. Continue roasting, basting occasionally, until the thigh juices run clear, about 30 minutes more. Remove the chicken from the oven and cover loosely with aluminum foil. Allow the chicken to rest for 10 to 15 minutes, then carve and serve sprinkled with coarse sea salt.

TRUSSING A CHICKEN
The classic method of trussing a chicken involves sewing the bird shut with a trussing needle and twine. I prefer the simpler method of tying the bird's cavity shut without sewing.

    To begin, cut a long piece of butcher's twine (available in most supermarkets), about 3 feet long, and loop the center around the narrowest part of each leg (the "ankles"), pulling the ends tightly to bind the legs together. Bring both ends of twine along the breast, nestling it between the breast and the legs, go around the outside of the wings with each end of the twine, then draw the string up to the nub at the chicken's neck. Cross the ends of the string over the nub. Holding both the strings and the nub, turn the bird over onto its breast. Tie the ends of the string into a tight knot at the nub of the neck.

pan-roasted striped bass

Any firm-fleshed fish (such as halibut, cod, snapper, salmon, grouper, etc.) may be substituted for the bass. Just make sure that the filets are about 1 inch thick or adjust the cooking time accordingly.

2 tablespoons peanut oil
4 1-inch-thick, center-cut striped bass
    fillets (6 ounces each), skin on
Kosher salt and freshly ground black
    pepper

3 to 4 tablespoons unsalted butter
2 sprigs of fresh thyme
Coarse sea salt

1. Heat the oil in a large skillet over medium heat until it slides easily across the pan. Dry the fillets thoroughly with paper towels, season them with kosher salt and pepper on both sides, then add them, skin-side down, to the skillet. Reduce the heat (the oil should sizzle, not sputter) and cook the fillets until the skins crisp, about 3 minutes. Turn the fillets and gently brown the other side, about 3 minutes more.

2. Add the butter and thyme. Continue cooking the fillets, turning them over once or twice (so that they brown evenly) and basting with the lightly browning butter. Cook until the fish is opaque, about 4 minutes more. Serve at once, drizzled with the browned butter and sprinkled with coarse sea salt.

THE SKIN OF THE FISH

Ask anyone what the best part of a fried chicken is and they'll tell you: the crispy, flavorful skin. The same holds true for the skin of the fish. I'm always amazed to see, when plates are cleared in my restaurants, how many people carefully peel the skin off and leave it aside. If you brown the skin correctly in the pan, it will form a delicious crisp crust, which I defy anyone to throw away! In order to cook the fillet evenly, though, remember to cook the skin side a little longer than the other, since the layer of fat just under the skin insulates the flesh and slows down the cooking.

pan-roasted sirloin

1 tablespoon peanut oil
1 (14-ounce) sirloin steak
    1½ to 2 inches thick, cut in half
    (see sidenote)
Kosher salt and freshly ground black
    pepper

2 tablespoons unsalted butter
2 sprigs of fresh thyme or rosemary
Coarse sea salt (optional)

1. Heat the oil in a small skillet over medium heat until it slides easily across the pan. Pat the steaks dry with paper towels. Season the steaks with kosher salt and pepper on both sides, then place them in the skillet. Reduce the heat slightly (the oil should sizzle, not sputter) and cook the steaks until the first sides are browned, about 3 minutes. Turn the steaks and brown the second sides, about 3 minutes more. Prop the steaks on their edges and brown the fat for about 2 minutes, then return the original sides of the steaks to the pan.

Rather than buying two individual steaks, buy one and cut it straight across the middle, so that you end up with two squarish medallions, each about 1½ to 2 inches thick. Cutting the steak this way will allow you to cook the meat longer over medium heat, giving you much more flavor and the nicely browned surface you want, without overcooking the center.

2. Cook the steaks for about another 2 minutes, then add the butter and herb sprigs. Continue turning the steaks from side to side, basting with the lightly browning butter until the steaks are done (a total of 13 to 15 minutes for medium rare). Remove the steaks from the skillet and allow them to rest for about 10 minutes. Slice and serve sprinkled with coarse sea salt.

Is it medium or medium rare? Here are two clear examples, with medium-rare on page 40 and medium on page 41.

Pan-roasted Sirloin with Pickled Ramps (recipe, page 195).

roasted herbed leg of lamb

SERVES 6 TO 8

1 (5-pound) boneless leg of lamb
Kosher salt and freshly ground black
    pepper
4 sprigs of fresh thyme
4 sprigs of fresh rosemary

4 sprigs of fresh sage
1 garlic clove, peeled and sliced
2 tablespoons peanut oil
2 to 3 tablespoons unsalted butter
Coarse sea salt

1. Heat the oven to 375°F. Lay the lamb out flat, cut-side up, on a clean surface. Sprinkle the meat with kosher salt and pepper, then arrange half of the thyme, rosemary, and sage and all of the garlic on the meat. Roll the meat around the herbs and tie with twine at 1-inch intervals.

2. Heat the oil in an ovenproof skillet or roasting pan over medium heat until it slides easily across the pan. Salt and pepper the outside of the lamb, then brown it on all sides, about 25 minutes. Transfer the skillet to the oven.

3. Cook the lamb for about 45 minutes. Add the butter and remaining herb sprigs and continue cooking the lamb, basting occasionally, for about 15 minutes. (The lamb is medium rare when a thermometer inserted in the center indicates an internal temperature of 125°F.) Remove the lamb from the oven, cover loosely with foil, and allow the meat to rest for about 10 minutes. Slice and serve sprinkled with coarse sea salt.

salt-roasted salmon

Although as a rule I prefer to roast at 350°F. or 375°F., salt roasting requires a slightly higher temperature, since the layer of salt insulates the fish from the heat.

1 tablespoon extra-virgin olive oil, plus
    additional for serving
1½ pounds center-cut salmon fillet
    (1¼ to 1½ inches thick), skin on,
    cut into 4 equal pieces

About 4 cups coarse sea salt
Freshly ground black pepper

1. Heat the oven to 400°F. Heat 1 tablespoon of oil in a medium ovenproof skillet over medium-high heat until it shimmers. Add the salmon, skin-side down, and cook until the skin begins to crisp, 2 to 3 minutes.

2. Mound the salt around and over each piece of salmon and roast in the oven for 6 minutes for medium-rare. Remove the salmon from the oven and carefully brush away the salt. (The top should look slightly rare but the sides cooked.) Transfer the salmon to a clean work surface and brush away the remaining salt. Season with freshly ground pepper and serve immediately drizzled with extra-virgin olive oil.

pan-roasted sweetbreads

SERVES 4 TO 6

You need to plan a bit ahead for this recipe, because the sweetbreads will be best if soaked overnight.

1 to 1½ pounds sweetbreads	1 tablespoon peanut oil
Kosher salt	3 tablespoons unsalted butter
About 1 cup flour	1 sprig of fresh thyme
Freshly ground black pepper	Coarse sea salt (optional)

1. Rinse the sweetbreads, then soak them in cold water in the refrigerator for at least 2 hours, preferably overnight.

2. Drain the sweetbreads, place them in a medium saucepan, cover with salted water, and bring to a simmer over medium heat. Simmer the sweetbreads for 2 minutes, then drain and rinse under cold water. Place the sweetbreads on a plate and chill for about an hour. Carefully remove as much of the outer membrane as you can without tearing the meat.

3. Lightly flour then season the sweetbreads with salt and pepper. Heat the oil in a large, heavy skillet over medium heat until it slides easily across the pan. Add the sweetbreads and cook for about 5 minutes. Turn the sweetbreads and reduce the heat to medium-low. Continue cooking, turning the sweetbreads so they brown on all sides and spooning off excess fat as you go, for about 7 minutes.

4. Add the butter and thyme and cook the sweetbreads, turning them occasionally and basting frequently with the butter, until they are crisp, nicely browned, and slightly firm, about 10 minutes more. Slice and serve sprinkled with coarse sea salt if desired.

The best sweetbreads are the thymus gland of a calf; they are only found in young animals (pig and lamb included), as the gland disappears with age. I love sweetbreads for their tenderness and neutral, delicate flavor, which make them an easy match with other foods. Roasting sweetbreads gives them a crispy exterior, while keeping the center creamy and moist. You can find sweetbreads at any good butcher or specialty food shop with a meat department.

pan-roasted soft-shell crabs with pickled ramps and crème fraîche

SERVES 4

This recipe illustrates how a basic pan-roasting technique can be used in conjunction with a vegetable component and a simple sauce to create a more evolved dish.

FOR THE SAUCE AND GARNISH
3 to 4 cups Pickled Ramps with pickling
 liquid (page 194)
3 tablespoons crème fraîche
Kosher salt and freshly ground black
 pepper

FOR THE CRABS
4 small to medium soft-shell crabs,
 cleaned by your fishmonger
1 tablespoon peanut oil
Kosher salt and freshly ground black
 pepper
1 tablespoon unsalted butter
1 tablespoon chopped fresh tarragon

1. **Preparing the sauce and garnish.** Strain the ramps, reserving ¾ cup of pickling liquid. Bring ½ cup of the liquid to a boil over medium-high heat in a small saucepan. Reduce the liquid until it is concentrated and slightly thickened (a glaze). Remove the pan from the heat and stir in a teaspoon of the remaining pickling liquid and the crème fraîche. Season with salt and pepper, and set it aside.

2. **Cooking the crabs.** Dry the crabs thoroughly with paper towels. Heat the oil in a large skillet over medium heat until it slides easily across the pan. Salt and pepper the crabs and place them in the skillet top-side down. Cook the crabs until they are crisp and slightly golden, about 2 minutes, then turn them and cook for 1 to 2 minutes more. Add the butter and tarragon and cook, basting the crabs with the tarragon butter, until the second side is crisp and the crabs are firm to the touch, about 1 minute. Drain on paper towels.

3. **Assembling the dish.** Warm the sauce over low heat. To serve, spoon the pickled ramps onto 4 plates, place the crabs on top of the ramps, then drizzle with the sauce.

pan-roasted lobster with bay leaf

SERVES 4

I love to cook lobster this way because the roasted flavor that results is rarely found in shellfish dishes. If you are squeamish about pulling apart live lobsters, blanch them for about 1 minute in boiling water; cool under cold, running water; and then pull the body apart from the tail.

4 (1¼-pound) live lobsters, tails and claws separated from bodies, bodies reserved for stock (page 71)
Kosher salt

1 tablespoon extra-virgin olive oil
Freshly ground black pepper
4 tablespoons unsalted butter
1 bay leaf

1. Wrap the lobster tails in a double layer of plastic wrap (this allows them to cook in their own juices for additional flavor). Place the tails and the claws in a pot of boiling salted water, weighting the tails (a heavy ceramic plate will work). Cover and boil for 4 minutes. Remove the tails to a plate and continue boiling the claws for an additional 3 minutes. Rinse the claws and tails under cold water, then crack them. Remove the meat.

2. Heat the olive oil in a large skillet over medium-high heat until it shimmers. Salt and pepper the lobster and add it to the pan. Cook the lobster for 30 seconds, then add 2 tablespoons of the butter and turn the lobster. Cook 30 seconds longer, then reduce the heat to low. Add the remaining 2 tablespoons of butter and the bay leaf and cook, turning the lobster in the butter, until the meat is just firm, about 3 minutes. Discard the bay leaf. Serve the lobster alone or with spiced lobster sauce (page 169) and Green Tomato Chutney (page 224).

pan-roasted salsify

Salsify is an autumn vegetable, with a slightly sweet flavor that some liken to an oyster, and a potato-like texture that lends itself well to roasting. Like a potato, salsify needs to be cooked slowly to keep it from becoming mushy. In this recipe, I accomplish this by braising the salsify gently in a little stock, which also adds a nice rich flavor, before roasting. Salsify is especially good with roasted meat and poultry.

2 lemons
1 pound salsify
4 cups chicken stock
Kosher salt and freshly ground black
    pepper

2 sprigs fresh thyme
1 tablespoon peanut oil
1 to 2 tablespoons butter

1. Combine the juice of the lemons and 2 quarts of water in a large bowl. Peel the salsify and place it in the lemon water so it doesn't brown.

2. Place the stock in a large saucepan. Drain the salsify and cut each stalk in half lengthwise, then into 3-inch lengths. Place the salsify in the stock, add salt, pepper, and thyme, and bring to a simmer over medium heat. Reduce the heat to medium-low and gently simmer until the salsify is tender, about 10 minutes. Allow the salsify to cool in the stock.

3. Drain the salsify (the braising liquid can be saved and reused). Dry the salsify with paper towels, and heat the oil in a large skillet over medium heat. Add the salsify and cook for 2 to 3 minutes, then add butter, salt, and pepper. Cook the salsify in the melting butter, turning occasionally, until it is golden brown on all sides, about 7 minutes. Serve immediately.

braising

WHEN I THINK OF BRAISED FOOD, WHAT COMES TO MIND are achingly rich, mellow flavors and meats so tender they melt in your mouth. Fish that falls apart on the fork, vegetables imbued with lush, complex flavor. Unlike some other techniques, which emphasize the individual components, braising creates dishes with such integrated flavors that it becomes hard to tell where the food ends and the sauce begins. At Gramercy Tavern, braised beef cheeks and braised pork belly are so rich and flavorful they have acquired a cultlike following normally reserved for foie gras.

Braising is a combination of two techniques: dry cooking initially (browning), then moist cooking, when the food is transferred to a pot with some liquid and cooked gently until finished. Each method teases a different quality from the finished dish.

Braised food is comfort food in the truest sense of the word.

If you learn to braise properly, you will have greatly expanded your cooking repertoire. Braising allows you to approach and cook a variety of secondary cuts of meat that you may have shied away from in the past. (This is also economical because these secondary cuts—like shanks, ribs, and shoulders—tend to be cheaper than their more tender counterparts.) The long slow cooking time of a braise is a perfect way to break down the collagen and sinew in these tougher cuts of meat, leaving behind a meltingly tender dish imbued with the flavors of the cooking liquid—usually stock or wine.

Fish also benefits from braising, although a typical fish braise is not as long a process; fish cooks faster, and there really are no secondary cuts of fish with tough connective tissue. As you'll see from the recipes that follow, I braise everything—including vegetables—

but the technique for each item is essentially the same. I like to teach braising, because I love the idea of a home cook walking the supermarket aisles and seeing each new item as an opportunity. Instead of thinking, Pork shoulder? What could I possibly do with that? You'll be thinking, Aha, pork shoulder. I'll braise it, and maybe add a few parsnips and turnips . . .

Another great thing about braising is that it yields a great sauce with a minimum of additional effort. Since braising involves cooking in aromatic liquid that gradually becomes imbued with the juices of the meat or fish being braised, this liquid—reduced slightly—makes a simple and intense sauce for the dish. The trick is to cook the food gently until it is very close to falling apart, to the point where it is difficult to transfer to the plate. The biggest mistake people make is to stop braising before this point, maybe because they have a fixation with neat food (I'm just guessing). Braised food is not neat food.

The simplicity of braising recipes appeals to me as well: Just before serving braised meat, or fish, you add whatever additional components you want in the dish. For example, as your braised salmon is almost finished cooking, you can add blanched peas, ramps, and morels, allowing them to finish cooking in the braising liquid. As they heat, they'll acquire some of the lush flavors of the fish and the liquid. When they're up to temperature, your entire dish is finished and ready to serve.

The other advantage to braising is that it is a wonderful make-ahead technique. Most meat braises are even better the second or third day, after the flavors have had a chance to further coalesce. To do this, simply transfer the braised meat from the braising dish into an ovenproof container. Strain the braising liquid and return it to the stove, then bring it to a simmer, skimming if necessary. Strain it again over the top of the meat and refrigerate (braised meat must be stored in its liquid or it will dry out). Later on, the next day, or even the day after that, simply place the entire dish into a 350° F. oven and reheat it gently, basting as necessary until heated through. At this point, if you want, you can add anything from cooked white beans to roasted tomatoes or sliced cooked artichokes—whatever you feel like—to create a richly flavored, complex dish.

basic braising technique

1. Brown the food in a skillet, in a small amount of oil. If your pan is not ovenproof, transfer the food to an ovenproof dish.

2. Add enough liquid to surround but not cover the food, transfer to the oven, and cook slowly, uncovered, at 250°F. to 350°F. In the oven, the liquid should be bubbling gently at a low simmer. **For fish:** Always transfer the fish to a new, ovenproof dish for this step, since the high temperature retained by the browning skillet will overcook the fish. For a "quick braise" of fish on top of the stove, the second pan need not be ovenproof.

3. You can serve the braised fish immediately; however, it is much better to allow braised meats to sit, refrigerated, for a day or two to develop more flavor and then gently reheat before serving. To do this, allow the meat to cool down in the braising liquid, or it will become dry (during this step the meat soaks up additional liquid). After it has cooled, pour off about three-quarters of the liquid through a chinois and reduce it over a low flame by about half until it is of sauce consistency, skimming constantly. (You will serve this sauce later with the braised meat.)

4. To reheat the braised meat: In the ovenproof dish, gently heat the food in the remaining braising liquid, basting it with the warm liquids from the pan. This will cause the outside of the meat to caramelize beautifully. When heated through, serve with the sauce.

braised short ribs

If you have difficulty finding fresh cherry peppers, you can use the grocery-store kind (which are in jars in the pickle section).

2 tablespoons peanut oil
Kosher salt and freshly ground black
    pepper
4 large, meaty beef short ribs (about
    4 pounds), cut in half
1 small onion, peeled and chopped
1 carrot, peeled and chopped
1 celery stalk, peeled and chopped

3 garlic cloves, unpeeled
5 sprigs of fresh thyme
8 fresh hot cherry peppers
½ cup sherry vinegar
2 to 3 cups Brown Chicken Stock
    (page 70)
2 sprigs of fresh tarragon

1. Heat the oven to 350°F. Heat the oil in a large deep oven-proof skillet over medium-high heat until it shimmers. Salt and pepper the ribs and cook them, in batches, until they are nicely browned on all sides, about 20 minutes.

Have your butcher cut each rib in half, since smaller ribs are easier to handle. This will leave you with 8 short ribs.

2. Remove the ribs and add the onion, carrot, celery, garlic, 2 sprigs of the thyme, and salt and pepper to the skillet. Cook, stirring occasionally, until the vegetables begin to soften, about 5 minutes, then add the peppers (if you are using canned peppers, add them with the vegetables in step 4). Continue cooking until the vegetables are tender and browned, 5 to 10 minutes more.

3. Return the ribs to the skillet. Add the vinegar and enough stock to come up the sides but not over the ribs. Bring the braising liquid to a simmer. Add the tarragon and the remaining thyme, then transfer the skillet to the oven and cook at a very gentle simmer (just an occasional bubble) for 1 hour. Turn the ribs and continue cooking until the meat is tender and comes easily away from the bone, about 1½ hours more.

4. Transfer the ribs and vegetables to a plate. Bring the braising liquid to a simmer and skim off the fat. Reduce the liquid slightly (just so it has a little body), then return the ribs and vegetables to the skillet. Simmer just long enough to reheat the ribs, then serve.

braised beef cheeks

You can buy beef cheeks from your local butcher, who will trim off the outer membrane and excess fat if you ask. I love beef cheeks because the rich, gelatinous meat is ideal for braising. This dish tends to elicit an especially passionate, primal response when I serve it in the restaurant, so prepare yourself if you're having guests.

3 tablespoons peanut oil
Kosher salt and freshly ground black
    pepper
4 beef cheeks (have your butcher trim
    the outer membrane and excess fat)
1 onion, peeled and chopped
2 carrots, peeled and chopped
1 leek, white part only, trimmed and
    chopped

2 celery stalks, peeled and chopped
3 garlic cloves, peeled
3 sprigs of fresh thyme
4 to 6 cups Brown Chicken Stock
    (page 70)
2 tablespoons unsalted butter (optional)

1. Heat the oven to 350°F. Heat the oil in a large ovenproof skillet over medium-high heat until it shimmers. Salt and pepper the beef cheeks, then brown them, about 10 minutes per side. Remove the beef from the skillet and set aside.

2. Add the onion, carrots, leek, celery, and garlic to the skillet, season with salt and pepper, and cook, stirring occasionally, until the vegetables soften, about 15 minutes. Add the thyme and return the beef to the skillet.

3. Pour in enough stock to surround but not cover the beef and bring it to a simmer. Transfer the skillet to the oven and cook the beef, uncovered, at a gentle simmer for 1 hour. Turn the beef and continue cooking until the meat is fork-tender, 1½ to 2 hours more.

4. Remove the beef from the skillet and set it aside. Strain the braising liquid and return it to the skillet. Bring the liquid to a simmer over medium heat and skim off the fat. Reduce the liquid by about half (it should have a little body), then return the beef to the skillet. Reheat the beef in the simmering broth, basting frequently. Stir in the butter (if using) and serve.

braised fresh "bacon"

SERVES 4

GQ magazine voted this their favorite meat dish of the year, after strenuous debate over whether I should call it "fresh bacon" or "pork belly." Whatever you want to call it, it is rich and delicious. When you buy pork belly, be sure to have your butcher leave the skin on.

1 tablespoon peanut oil
Kosher salt and freshly ground black
    pepper
2 pounds pork belly, skin on
1 onion, peeled and coarsely chopped
2 carrots, peeled and coarsely
    chopped

2 celery stalks, peeled and coarsely
    chopped
1 leek, white part only, trimmed and
    chopped
2 garlic cloves, peeled
About 3 cups Brown Chicken Stock
    (page 70)

1. Heat the oven to 350° F. Heat the oil in a large ovenproof skillet over medium heat until the oil slides easily across the pan. Salt and pepper the pork and add it, fat-side down, to the skillet. Cook until the skin is browned, about 15 minutes, then transfer the pork to a plate.

2. Pour off all but about 2 tablespoons of fat and add the onion, carrots, celery, leek, and garlic to the skillet. Cook the vegetables, stirring occasionally, until they are tender and beginning to brown, about 20 minutes. Return the pork belly to the skillet, fat-side up, and add about 2 cups of stock (it should surround but not cover the meat). Bring the stock to a simmer, then transfer the skillet to the oven. Gently simmer the pork, uncovered, for 1 hour, then add another cup of stock. Continue cooking until the pork is tender enough to cut with a fork, about 1 hour longer.

3. Allow the pork to cool in the braising liquid. Remove the pork from the liquid, then gently lift off and discard the skin (use a small knife to separate any pieces that don't come away from the fat easily). Score the fat, making crosshatch incisions, then cut the pork into 4 equal pieces.

4. Increase the oven to 400° F. Strain the braising liquid, discarding the solids. Return the liquid to the skillet, bring it to a simmer, and skim off the fat. Return

pork, fat-side up, to the skillet. Transfer the skillet to the oven and cook, without basting, until the pork is heated through and the fat nicely browned, about 20 minutes. Serve the pork in a shallow bowl moistened with a bit of the braising liquid.

braised red snapper

SERVES 4 AS A FIRST COURSE OR 2 AS A MAIN

1 red bell pepper
1 lemon
1 pound red snapper fillet (skin on)
Kosher salt and freshly ground black
    pepper

1 tablespoon extra-virgin olive oil
About ¼ cup Lemon–Rosemary
    Vinaigrette (page 83)
1 or 2 tablespoons chopped fresh
    flat-leaf parsley

1. Char the pepper over an open-burner flame, then place it in a sealed plastic container until cool enough to handle. Gently scrape away the charred skin, discard the stem and seeds, and cut out the veins. Cut the pepper into strips.

2. Peel and remove any pith from the lemon (discard the pith but reserve the peel for another purpose). Divide the lemon into segments and set aside.

3. Dry the snapper fillet thoroughly with paper towels, then cut it crosswise into 4 equal pieces. Salt and pepper the fish. Heat the oil over medium heat in a medium skillet, add the fish, skin-side down, and cook it until the skin crisps, about 3 minutes. Remove the fish, wipe out the skillet, and let it cool.

4. Place the pepper strips and lemon segments in the skillet. Add enough vinaigrette to cover the bottom of the skillet (the vinaigrette should surround, not cover, the lemons and peppers). Nestle the fish, skin-side up, among the peppers and lemons. Bring the vinaigrette to a simmer over medium heat and cook, basting the fish frequently, until it flakes easily, about 3 minutes. Sprinkle with parsley and serve.

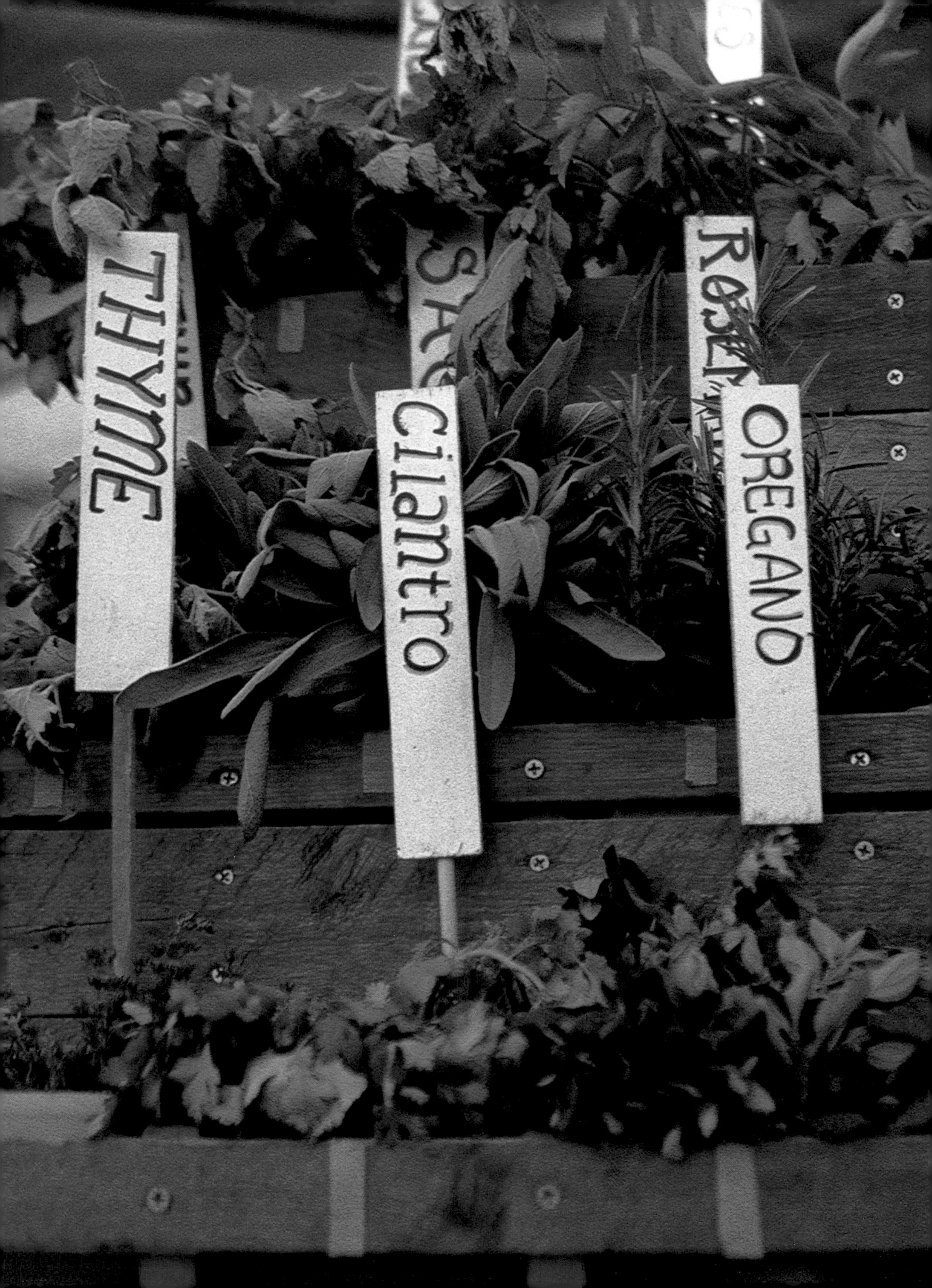
THYME
Cilantro
OREGANO

FRESH HERBS

Years after I started cooking I learned the difference between fresh herbs and dried; as far as I can tell the drying process changes the essential flavor of the herb (dried thyme, for example, tastes nothing to me like fresh). The stronger flavors of dried herbs seem jarring to me, as well. I prize fresh herbs for their vegetal delicacy and nuance, qualities that go out the door once an herb is dried. You'll notice that just about all of the recipes in this book call for fresh herbs.

In my restaurants and at home I use herbs to flavor braises, or add them to butter to baste meat and fish. Often I'll chop fresh herbs and stuff them under the skin of a chicken before roasting. A mixture of herbs with delicate textures—like chervil, basil, parsley, and chive—can make a small flavorful salad all on its own, which pairs nicely with roasted fish or marinated salmon. A handful of herbs, blanched and puréed, then added to beurre fondue makes a vibrant, elemental sauce. Although the recipes throughout this book suggest specific herbs—thyme with Pan-Roasted Striped Bass, for example—these are not hard-and-fast rules. If you have a pot of rosemary growing on the windowsill, use that instead. Whatever is on hand that is fresh will work and be delicious.

Nowadays, fresh herbs can be purchased in just about any good supermarket. Although most recipes call for only one sprig or two, don't be deterred by the size of a package of supermarket herbs. Buy the whole thing and use liberally; unlike dried, you run little risk of overpowering a dish with most fresh herbs. To wash, dip herbs into a bowl of cool water or under a thin stream of tap water. Always use a very sharp knife to chop herbs and do so only at the last moment—never in advance.

blanching

bLANCHING IS ONE OF THOSE TECHNIQUES THAT FEW CHEFS talk about—it lacks the drama of roasting and the nuance of braising—yet it is one of those techniques that figures importantly in my cooking because of my reliance on fresh vegetables. It is easy to do once you learn a few tricks, and it will help you to have the components on hand to build both simple and complex recipes.

Blanching is the technique of cooking food briefly in a large amount of rapidly boiling, salted water. Blanching vegetables quickly allows them to retain their essential cell structure, so they don't turn limp, and it keeps the chlorophyll in the cells, which is how green vegetables maintain their vibrant color.

The great benefit to blanching vegetables in advance is that it allows you to get some of the cooking out of the way in order to focus on the rest of the recipe. This is especially helpful in a restaurant setting, where we blanch our vegetables early in the afternoon, refrigerate them, then take them out as needed throughout the night. As we rush to prepare intricate dishes in a limited amount of time, all we need to do is heat the vegetables as they are incorporated into the dish. It saves us lots of time and allows us to really control the cooking process.

This same technique also benefits the home cook. Once your guests have arrived, for example, you can add blanched vegetables to the roasting pan as your chicken finishes cooking. The vegetables will acquire the rich, roasted flavors of the chicken and become an integrated part of the dish. As you read this book, you'll find many recipes that call for blanched vegetables as an ingredient. The assumption is that you will read the recipe and blanch the peas (or ramps, or asparagus) ahead of time, thereby freeing you up to focus on the gestalt of the dish.

A vegetable should be cooked until the crunch is just gone but the resistance remains.

basic blanching technique

1. Bring a large pot of salted water to a roiling boil. Have a large bowl of ice water standing by. The salt is important, as it, too, helps green vegetables retain their chlorophyll. You need a large amount of water, so that the temperature doesn't drop when you add the vegetables.

2. Add the vegetables to the boiling water. If you have a large amount, blanch them in two batches to keep the temperature of the water up. Do not cover the pot, as it will make the vegetables lose their color.

3. Remove the vegetables with a slotted spoon when they are just cooked through—a couple of minutes at the most—and plunge into the ice water to arrest the cooking.

4. Drain the vegetables as soon as they have cooled down. Place into a covered container and refrigerate for later use.

For an example of a recipe that begins with basic blanched vegetables, see Summer Vegetable Ragout (page 206).

A BRIEF TIRADE ABOUT UNDERCOOKED VEGETABLES

As nouvelle cuisine became popular in the late seventies, French chefs made much of "undercooking" their vegetables. American chefs adopted this practice and began undercooking vegetables, too, leaving them hard and raw in the center. What we were all missing was the reference point from which the French chefs had begun: For generations European chefs cooked vegetables to the point of mush, to accommodate teeth that had never known the benefit of fluoridated water, as Americans' had. When the French chefs "undercooked" vegetables, they were finally cooking them correctly; just through and no more. I was guilty of undercooking vegetables myself once, cooking everything *al dente* and missing out on the flavor of properly cooked vegetables! Years later, after spending time in France, I learned that a perfectly cooked vegetable—be it a carrot or cauliflower—should be cooked until the crunch is just gone but the resistance remains. No more . . . and no less.

stock-making

STOCKS ARE THE BASIS FOR SAUCES AND SOUPS AND IMPORTANT flavoring agents for braises. Admittedly, stock-making is time consuming, but the extra effort yields great dividends. In my restaurants I make a separate stock for each dish (rabbit stock, venison stock, fish stock, and so on) because I like to heighten and articulate the flavor of each food with a sauce or *jus* of itself. This is excessive when you're cooking at home; a basic white and brown chicken stock and veal stock will give you plenty of options. But if space or time limitations dictate that you have only one on hand, the brown chicken stock will do.

Making a good stock is not difficult. I recommend that you make a big batch when you have some time and then freeze it in small containers or sealable bags for later use (let it cool in the refrigerator first). Stock should keep in the freezer for about four months.

An important rule of stock-making can be summed up like this: Garbage in, garbage out. Too many people view stocks as an opportunity to get rid of odds and ends, things that have been sitting around that they might otherwise throw out. This will compromise the quality of the stock. Always use fresh high-quality bones, vegetables, and herbs for the best flavor. Freshness is as important in making a stock as it is in preparing a main course.

All of these recipes call for the addition of a mixture of coarsely chopped carrots, celery, onions, and leeks, known as **mirepoix** (sometimes referred to as aromatics). Exact proportions are not crucial here; for five gallons of stock, one small carrot, one or two small celery stalks, one or two small leeks, and one small onion are about right. The term "mirepoix" actually refers to the cut—rough, and approximately the size of your thumbnail. A tiny, fine dice of vegetables is called *brunoise*, and is not necessary here.

The last step for any stock is to strain the liquid, to remove any particles of vegetables and herbs. I recommend straining through a fine strainer (also called a chinois).

white chicken stock

A white chicken stock is the first step toward making brown chicken stock: it also has many uses of its own. White chicken stock cannot be made with the leftover bones from a roasted chicken (save those for brown chicken stock). Instead, purchase the bones from your local butcher, who will be happy to sell them to you cheap. If you can't find chicken bones, substitute about 4 pounds of chicken legs, wings, and backs.

4 pounds chicken bones or 4 pounds
    chicken legs, wings, and backs
1 onion, peeled and quartered
1 carrot, peeled and coarsely
    chopped
2 stalks celery, coarsely chopped

2 leeks, white parts only, trimmed and
    chopped
1 bay leaf
Peppercorns
3 to 4 sprigs fresh flat-leaf parsley
3 to 4 sprigs fresh thyme

1. Rinse chicken bones or chicken parts well. Remove the fat and skin if any, and place into a pot with just enough hot water to cover. Bring to a boil over medium-high heat and let boil for about 2 minutes.

2. Drain the chicken and discard the water (see sidenote). Return the chicken to the pot, cover with fresh water and bring to a simmer over medium-high heat. Reduce the heat to medium and gently simmer the stock for about 1 hour, skimming whenever fat or scum accumulates on the surface. Add more hot water if necessary to keep the level consistent.

Pouring off the original water after the first boil will remove all of the blood and a lot of the coagulated proteins, which form a gray scum on the surface. Classic technique allows you to merely skim this off the surface, adding more water if necessary. I prefer to update that method in this way, since no matter how much you skim, you'll never be rid of the byproducts completely. Don't worry that you're throwing out flavor, you're not. The bones need to cook a good deal longer to extract flavor.

3. Add the onion, carrot, celery, leeks, bay leaf, and peppercorns. Simmer for 15 minutes. Add the parsley and thyme and simmer for an additional 5 minutes. Take the pot off the heat and strain the stock. Cool, and refrigerate for up to 5 days or freeze for up to 4 months.

Definition: When I say simmer, I mean a low, gentle boil.

brown chicken stock

Brown chicken stock forms the base for many sauces and braises and is an essential ingredient to have at the ready in your kitchen (it freezes well). Although you could use water in place of white chicken stock, I don't recommend it. The results are far superior—richer flavor and fuller texture—when you use white chicken stock instead.

4 pounds chicken bones or 4 pounds
  chicken legs, wings, and backs (see
  headnote on page 69)
2 tablespoons peanut oil
White Chicken Stock (page 69)
1 to 2 teaspoons tomato paste
1 onion, peeled and quartered
1 carrot, peeled and coarsely chopped

2 stalks celery, coarsely chopped
2 leeks, white parts only, trimmed and
  chopped
1 bay leaf
3 to 4 sprigs fresh flat-leaf parsley
1 sprig fresh thyme
1 sprig fresh rosemary

1. Rinse the bones or chicken well and remove as much fat and skin as possible.

2. Heat the oil in a large pot over medium heat. Add the chicken and brown, turning, until golden brown. Be careful not to burn the bones (see sidenote).

3. Place the browned chicken into a stockpot and cover by about an inch with white chicken stock. Add the tomato paste and bring to a simmer. Cook for 1 hour, skimming whenever fat or scum accumulates on the surface.

4. Add the onion, carrot, celery, leeks, and bay leaf and continue to cook for another 15 minutes. Add the parsley, thyme, and rosemary and cook for another 5 minutes. Strain. Return the stock to the pot and simmer over medium heat until reduced by half. Allow to cool, then refrigerate for up to 5 days or freeze for up to 4 months.

BROWNING THE BONES

When browning the bones, it is very important not to burn them. Even the smallest bit of burnt matter will cause the stock to turn bitter.

You do not need to aim for a very dark color and risk burning the bones: The color of the stock doesn't come from the browned bones, as most people assume, but from the tomato paste, added later. Lightly browning the bones will be sufficient to lend a roasted flavor to the stock.

lobster stock

MAKES ABOUT 3 CUPS

I rely on lobster stock as a basis for lobster sauce and lobster risotto (page 172). As with chicken stock or veal stock, I recommend making more than you'll need and freezing the extra.

If you are squeamish about pulling apart live lobsters, blanch them for about 1 minute in boiling water; cool under cold, running water; and then pull apart the body from the tail.

4 lobster bodies, split lengthwise
2 tablespoons extra-virgin olive oil
1 onion, peeled and chopped
1 leek, white part only, trimmed and chopped

1 carrot, peeled and chopped
1 celery stalk, chopped
1 sprig of fresh thyme

1. Remove the head sack, tomalley, and roe from the lobster bodies (discard the head sack but freeze the tomalley and roe for another use). Break or cut the bodies into 4 to 6 pieces each.

2. Heat the oil in a large pot over medium-low heat until it spreads over the bottom of the pan. Add the onion, leek, carrot, and celery and cook, stirring occasionally, until the vegetables are tender, about 20 minutes. Add the lobster bodies and thyme and cook, stirring frequently, until the lobster shells begin to turn red, about 5 minutes. Add water to cover, about 6 cups, and gently simmer, skimming as needed, until the stock is flavorful, about 1 hour. Ladle the stock through a fine sieve and set aside to cool. Store the stock in the refrigerator for up to 1 week or in the freezer for up to 6 months.

veal stock

I like the rich meat flavor of veal stock, which I use as a basis for saucing many meat dishes and braises. To make veal stock, follow the same two-step process as for Brown Chicken Stock: Start with a white veal stock, then add veal bones and tomato paste to make a brown stock, and reduce by half. The only difference here is that you should not attempt to brown the veal bones, which are large and unwieldy and burn easily. Simply cook them longer, as the recipe instructs, to extract their full flavor.

The color of the stock doesn't come from the browned bones, as most people assume, but from the tomato paste.

4 pounds veal bones
1 onion, peeled and quartered
1 carrot, peeled and coarsely chopped
2 stalks celery, coarsely chopped
2 leeks, white parts only, trimmed and
    chopped

2 bay leaves
5 to 6 peppercorns, or to taste
Fresh sprigs of thyme and fresh herbs of
    your choice (such as flat-leaf parsley
    or rosemary)
3 tablespoons tomato paste

1. Rinse half the veal bones well, removing as much fat and skin as possible. Place into a pot with just enough hot water to cover.

2. Bring to a boil, and let it boil for about 2 minutes.

3. Drain the bones and discard the water. This will remove all of the blood and a lot of the coagulated proteins, which form a gray scum on the surface (see side-note, page 69).

4. Return the bones to the pot and cover by about 1 inch with hot water. Bring to a simmer, skimming whatever new fat or scum accumulates on the surface. Simmer for about 2 hours, adding more hot water, if necessary, to keep the level consistent. Continue to skim the surface until by-products no longer appear.

5. Add half the vegetables, 1 of the bay leaves, and the peppercorns. Simmer for an additional 15 minutes.

6. Add a sprig each of the thyme and the other fresh herbs of your choice and cook for an additional 5 minutes. Take the pot off the heat and strain the stock.

7. Place the remaining veal bones into a clean stockpot. Add the veal stock. It should come up an inch over the bones (add water if necessary). Add the tomato paste. Bring to a simmer.

8. Simmer for 2 hours, skimming whatever fat or scum accumulates on the surface.

9. Add the remaining vegetables and bay leaf and continue to cook for another 15 minutes.

10. Add a sprig each of the thyme and fresh herbs and cook for another 5 minutes.

11. Remove from the heat and strain.

12. Return the stock to the pot and simmer over medium heat until reduced by half. Allow to cool, then refrigerate for up to 5 days or freeze for up to 4 months.

sauce-making

S OME PEOPLE WOULD PREFER TO THINK OF SAUCE-MAKING AS some mysterious all-day process, the exclusive province of temperamental chefs and the French, but nothing could be further from the truth. In many cases, a sauce is simply a little bit of stock reinforced with flavoring agents like vinegar, wine, horseradish, or herbs, depending on the dish. The technique is easy and varies little from sauce to sauce, the only variables being the ingredients you choose.

basic sauce-making technique

Take, for example, sherry wine vinegar sauce. As with any sauce, you begin with a small amount of mirepoix (see page 68).

1. Sweat the vegetables in a small amount of oil until soft.

2. Add some sherry wine vinegar (or red wine vinegar for red wine vinegar sauce, balsamic for balsamic vinegar sauce . . . you get the picture).

3. Reduce until there is very little liquid left, being sure to lower the heat as you go so that the liquid doesn't burn.

4. Once the liquid is nearly gone and the vegetables appear mostly dry, **add the stock.**

5. Bring the whole thing up to a simmer, skim, then **reduce it,** over medium heat, to the consistency you want.

6. Last, **strain** the entire mixture through a fine strainer, and *voilà,* you have a sauce.

Once you've got the basic technique down, you simply manipulate the variables to create different sauces. Bordelaise sauce? Start with red wine, shallots, and a little thyme. Reduce it until nearly gone, and add veal stock. Reduce again to the desired consistency and strain through a fine chinois.

To make sauce for different meat dishes, purchase the appropriate bones from your butcher and follow the same basic technique. Venison sauce? Sweat some mirepoix and add to browned venison bones. Add the flavoring agent of your choice—I like red wine, juniper berries, rosemary, and orange zest—and reduce it until almost dry. Add some veal stock; reduce again, then strain. Duck sauce? Save or buy duck bones, use brown chicken stock instead, and follow the same technique. A good rule of thumb is to use brown chicken stock for poultry dishes, veal stock for meat-based dishes.

beurre fondue

The term "fondue" tends to confuse people, conjuring an image of bubbling cheese in a dipping pot. Fondue is actually French for "melted," and refers to anything melted in water. Beurre fondue is butter melted in water, a technique many cooks rely upon to keep butter in a creamy, emulsified state that makes it easy to use and less greasy on the palate.

Buerre fondue has numerous uses; it is easier than whole butter for basting meats or braising fish, and is especially useful when I need to add richness and a round but neutral flavor to seafood like crab or sea urchin. Beurre fondue can form the basis for a simple vegetable ragout and is the perfect medium for quickly reheating blanched vegetables. Vegetables with a pat of melting butter is as classic a dish as I know, but substituting beurre fondue keeps that "pat" of butter from separating and tasting greasy. My cooks in the restaurants each have a small container of beurre fondue on hand, which they use throughout the night.

This is a good place to bring up how I feel about butter: I like butter. Butter is good.

There really is no substitute for the flavor of butter, and as you've noticed, I use it generously in my cooking. In short, it is a conduit for flavor—and I tend to go for any method that gives me optimal flavor.

basic beurre fondue technique

1. Bring about ½ inch of water to a simmer in a small saucepan.

2. Start adding butter, about a tablespoon at a time, whisking to melt. As the beurre fondue reaches a gentle simmer, you may notice small oil droplets starting to form. This is a sign that the water is beginning to evaporate, so add a small amount of warm water to compensate.

3. Keep adding butter until you have incorporated ¾ cup into the sauce, making sure not to add too much too quickly, as this will lower the temperature in the pot and cause the sauce to solidify.

4. Keep in a warm place. Once made, beurre fondue must be kept warm or it will start to separate. A bain-marie usually does the trick: Fill a larger pot or metal container with warm water and set the pot with the beurre fondue into that. Keep the entire thing near the stove where you are working.

beurre blanc

Beurre blanc is a classic butter sauce. Although the recipes in this book don't expressly call for beurre blanc, any discussion of sauces and butter sauces would be incomplete without it. Beurre blanc uses the same technique as beurre fondue, but a different liquid stabilizer. Beurre blanc makes a simple delicious sauce for roasted fish.

¼ cup white wine vinegar
¼ cup white wine
2 shallots, finely chopped

½ pound (2 sticks) unsalted butter
Kosher salt and freshly ground black
   pepper

1. Combine the vinegar, wine, and shallots in a small saucepan. Bring to a simmer over medium heat and reduce until the pan is almost dry.

2. Return the heat to low and add the butter, 1 tablespoon at a time, whisking continuously to incorporate. Do not add the butter too quickly, as this will lower the temperature and cause the sauce to separate.

3. Strain the sauce through a fine strainer, add salt and pepper, and keep warm over very low heat until you're ready to use it.

apple cider sauce

This sauce takes the basic technique one step further, adding and reducing chicken stock, then thickening the reduction with butter. I love to serve this sauce over Brussels Sprouts with Bacon (page 246).

½ cup apple cider
½ cup cider vinegar
2 tablespoons Brown Chicken Stock
   (page 70)
1 small shallot, peeled and finely
   chopped

1 sprig of fresh thyme
¼ pound (1 stick) unsalted butter, cut
   into 6 to 8 pieces
Kosher salt and freshly ground black
   pepper

1. Place the cider, vinegar, stock, shallot, and thyme in a small saucepan. Bring to a boil over medium-high heat, lower the heat to medium, and reduce by half, about 5 minutes.

2. Reduce the heat to low and whisk in the butter a piece at a time. Strain the sauce, add salt and pepper, and keep warm over very low heat until ready to use.

VINAIGRETTES

I like the versatility of a vinaigrette, which I use as a braising liquid or light sauce for fish, or to dress cold dishes and salads. Over the past few years, chefs have started to use flavored vinaigrettes as an alternative to the heavy sauces of traditional French cuisine.

There are two basic kinds of vinaigrette: emulsified and unemulsified. Emulsified vinaigrette—which has the creamy appearance of a light mayonnaise—is created by whisking oil into vinegar until the vinegar particles surround the oil, giving the appearance of having "blended" into a creamy sauce. A little bit of protein added to the mix —like an egg or a bit of chicken stock—will assist the process. For this reason, flavoring a vinaigrette almost always makes it easier to emulsify. Unemulsified vinaigrettes, which have a less creamy, pellucid appearance, are made without the addition of protein.

I usually make my vinaigrettes in a blender, starting with the vinegar, salt and pepper, and a flavoring agent like roasted tomatoes or lemons and rosemary and then slowly adding oil with the blender on a slow speed. In place of the blender, you can easily mix vinaigrette by hand; just make sure to whisk in one direction only, and add the oil slowly to assist the emulsification.

basic vinaigrette

1 shallot, peeled and diced
½ teaspoon Dijon mustard
¼ cup white wine vinegar
Kosher salt and freshly ground black
    pepper

½ cup extra-virgin olive oil
½ cup canola oil

Combine the shallot, mustard, vinegar, and salt and pepper to taste in a small bowl. Whisking constantly, gradually add the olive oil and canola oil.

truffle vinaigrette

Black truffles are in season from late fall through spring (see Resources for information on ordering truffles, page 266) and they lend a combination of elegance and earthiness to any dish. To make truffle vinaigrette, simply add about 2 tablespoons finely chopped black truffles to half the Basic Vinaigrette recipe. I like to use truffle vinaigrette, at room temperature, as a simple sauce for roasted monkfish.

tomato vinaigrette

This vinaigrette makes a great sauce for roasted fish, or use it to dress sliced raw tomatoes in the summertime.

¼ cup chopped, roasted tomato halves
  (page 92)
½ teaspoon Dijon mustard
¼ cup white wine vinegar

½ cup extra-virgin olive oil
½ cup canola oil
Kosher salt and freshly ground black
  pepper

Place the tomatoes, mustard, and vinegar into a blender. Blend at low speed, adding the oils in a thin stream. Strain the vinaigrette. Season to taste with salt and pepper. Serve as is, or thin slightly with a little of the liquid from the roasted tomatoes.

lemon–rosemary vinaigrette

This vinaigrette works especially well served with an eggplant "napoleon"—a dish I make by layering Pan-Fried Eggplant (page 210) and Eggplant Caviar (page 209).

2 tablespoons white wine vinegar
2 tablespoons fresh lemon juice
1 sprig of fresh rosemary, leaves picked
  and chopped

Zest of 1 lemon, finely chopped
Kosher salt and freshly ground black
  pepper
⅓ cup extra-virgin olive oil

Combine the vinegar, lemon juice, rosemary, lemon zest, and salt and pepper in a small bowl. Whisking constantly, gradually add the olive oil.

Curly Endive
ⓒⓡⓞ ⓒⓡⓞ
☆ A MILD. BITTER SALAD
$ 2.00

HOW TO
CHOOSE INGREDIENTS

I have the simplest tastes. I am always satisfied with the best.

—Oscar Wilde

Ever wonder why an entrée of grilled tuna costs eighteen dollars in one restaurant and thirty dollars in another? There is a vast difference in the quality (and price point) of ingredients available to chefs, who in turn pass these costs on to the diner. Surprisingly, the more expensive stuff is often a better value, because the chef is unwilling to place as high a markup on the item. In the interest of serving the best quality, he will "eat" the difference in price.

Ingredients produced by small producers, in smaller batches, tend toward a higher quality. In my restaurants, Gramercy Tavern and Craft, I shoot for the best ingredients I can get, for every step of the cooking process, since even the smallest hint of flavor in a dish is too important to ignore. The quality differential between mass-produced vinegars and artisanal vinegars, for example, is apparent at first taste: It is the difference between harsh, acerbic notes and carefully nuanced, balanced acidity. The same holds true for small producers of olive oil, who invest time, money, and expertise in growing premium fruit and producing tiny batches. The resulting flavors and bouquet can, quite literally, transform a dish.

This is especially true with vegetables. When choosing vegetables, think like an Italian peasant: Even an Italian of the most modest means will spend a few extra lire on the best tomato, the freshest herbs, the fruitiest olive oil. If you've ever eaten a simple tomato salad in Italy, you know what I mean.

What I'm getting at is that you should always buy the best you can afford. These ingredients aren't more expensive because they're trendy or have a chic label. In fact, in the case of condiments, you will find yourself using less because the flavors are more intense and go farther.

studies

creating "ingredients"

Ideas are like rabbits. You get a couple, learn how to handle them, and pretty soon you have a dozen.

—John Steinbeck

GREAT MOMENTS OF CREATIVITY CAN USUALLY BE TRACED back to a few simple sparks—often mundane—that set off a chain of events, elevating everything that follows. Take the Italian Renaissance painters who one day switched from temperas bonded with plaster to oils on canvas. Suddenly European painters could spend days or weeks painting a hand instead of having to finish before the plaster set, and a revolution in detail and depth was begun.

I feel the same concept applies to cooking, though perhaps with less historical consequence. Often, if you can get one good idea working, it sets the stage for many others. Growth becomes a matter of building around that initial idea and seeing how far you can take it.

These initial ideas usually revolve around vegetables. Believe it or not, I rarely begin with the thought, Gee, I've got some beef. How should I serve it? The proteins—beef, lamb, chicken, fish—are the constants. What do change frequently, bringing the color and excitement of the changing seasons, are the vegetables. So, vegetables make up the building blocks that spark our imagination and let us fly.

Tomatoes are a good example. Around the end of the summer we are faced with a huge abundance of ripe, juicy tomatoes, and it feels like a shame to waste them. Some become a sauce (a.k.a. gravy in my mother's house), but I love the concentrated flavor of roasted tomatoes, so I roast a bunch with a little garlic and thyme. Now that I have a batch of roasted tomatoes, they become a basic "ingredient," and the question becomes, How can I use them? Then it's a matter of manipulating the ingredient with a variety of techniques, each building on the last, to create interesting dishes.

For example, to keep it simple, I could toss the roasted tomatoes with some fresh herbs, olive oil, and pasta. Or, building on the pasta idea, I could roughly chop the tomatoes and use them as a filling for ravioli. I can purée the roasted tomatoes, add some vinegar, then emulsify the mixture with oil to make a vinaigrette that I'll use to dress a salad of fresh greens and seared tuna. As I get more ambitious, I can roll a fillet of sea bass around the roasted tomatoes, wrap the whole thing in sheer caul fat, and roast that. Or I can use them with braised lamb, adding them with white beans in the final stage of the braise. The ideas just keep coming. Whether I harness them in a few simple ways, or keep building idea upon idea to yield something more complex, the same basic ingredient—roasted tomatoes—is the starting point.

To truly understand how a chef thinks, it's important to grasp this concept: I am always thinking outward, from one idea to many. From simple to complex. I rarely start out thinking in terms of the finished dish, that is, "Today I will make Braised Lamb Shanks with White Beans in Roasted Tomato Broth." Instead I start with the essentials: "I've got these gorgeous tomatoes; they might be nice with those lamb shanks in the walk-in."

I started this book with the chapter on techniques because without the fundamental methods at your disposal, the process I've just described becomes difficult to execute. But once you have roasting, braising, blanching, stock-making, and sauce-making at your fingertips, you can extrapolate outward from the basic components: tomatoes, lamb shanks, white beans. All it takes is a little practice, which is why this chapter presents three different studies, each based upon an underlying "ingredient"—roasted tomatoes, pan-roasted mushrooms, and braised artichokes—to give you a chance to work this concept yourself.

I hope you'll start thinking this way as you walk the market, seeing food as simple ingredients from which to build. You might even find yourself steering clear of a recipe altogether, to experiment with the ingredient by layering it with the foods you like best. You will be "authoring" your own recipes and thinking like a chef.

roasted
tomatoes

EVERYBODY KNOWS THE BEST TOMATOES COME FROM NEW Jersey. When I was growing up, we lived in an urban neighborhood in Elizabeth (I thought "countryside" meant the suburbs until I was fourteen). Nonetheless, we had a tomato vine growing in a small patch of garden sowed between the fences of our backyard. Come late summer, there were more tomatoes than we knew what to do with.

My grandmother would make tomato purée that she would can in mason jars and use all winter long. But as I started to work in my own kitchens, I hit on another way to make the tomato harvest of late summer last longer: Simply roast the tomatoes with a little garlic and thyme, which removes most of the water and intensifies the flavor. They freeze easily and can be used all winter. These roasted tomatoes are not as dehydrated as the sun-dried variety that seem to be every-where (they also don't require reconstituting) and they perfectly illus-trate the concept of starting with one "ingredient" and building outward, from simple to increasingly complex. The leftover roasted garlic, incidentally, has a creamy, mellow flavor not found in the raw vegetable and makes a great spread on a piece of crusty bread.

Roasted tomatoes perfectly illustrate the concept of starting with one "ingredient" and building outward, from simple to complex.

a word about tomatoes

Although you can get tomatoes year-round, I recommend them only—at least here in the Northeast—in late summer. I suggest you seek out tomatoes that are locally grown; they ripen longer on the vine, instead of being picked early to ripen during shipping. Store tomatoes stem-side down and never refrigerate.

roasted tomatoes and garlic

MAKES 40 ROASTED TOMATO HALVES, APPROXIMATELY 20 ROASTED GARLIC CLOVES, AND 1 TO 3 CUPS ROASTED TOMATO JUICE

Roasting intensifies the flavor of even less-than-spectacular tomatoes, in case local greenmarket varieties are unavailable.

20 ripe tomatoes, stems and cores removed
2 large heads of garlic divided into unpeeled cloves

½ cup extra-virgin olive oil
Kosher salt and freshly ground black pepper
8 sprigs of fresh thyme

1. Heat the oven to 350° F. Cut the tomatoes in half cross-wise (through the equator), then place the tomatoes, garlic, and olive oil in a large bowl. Season with salt and pepper and mix gently. Line two large, rimmed baking sheets with parchment paper or aluminum foil. Place the tomato halves on the baking sheets, cut-side down, and then pour any olive oil left in the bowl over them. Divide the garlic and thyme between the baking sheets and bake until the tomato skins loosen, about 20 minutes.

This recipe leaves you with three distinct, usable parts:

1. The roasted tomato
2. The tomato liquid
3. The roasted garlic

They provide the cornerstone for all of the following recipes.

2. Remove and discard the tomato skins. Pour any juices that have accumulated into a bowl and reserve. Return the tomatoes to the oven and reduce the temperature to 275° F. Continue roasting, periodically pouring off and reserving the juices, until the tomatoes are slightly shrunken and appear cooked and concentrated but not yet dry, 3 to 4 hours more. Remove the tomatoes from the oven and allow them to cool on the baking sheets. Discard the thyme and transfer the tomatoes and garlic to separate containers. Store the tomatoes, garlic, and reserved tomato juices in the refrigerator for up to 1 week or in the freezer for up to 6 months.

1. Slice tomatoes in half.

2. Lay, cut-side down, on sheet pan with garlic, olive oil, and thyme.

3. Remove skins after cooking.

4. Store juices and tomatoes in separate containers.

roasted tomato, zucchini, and eggplant lasagne

SERVES 6

½ cup ricotta cheese
1 small onion, peeled
2 small zucchini
½ medium eggplant
1 red bell pepper, peeled and seeded
4 tablespoons extra-virgin olive oil
1 garlic clove, peeled and sliced
Kosher salt and freshly ground black
    pepper

1 bay leaf
2 sprigs of fresh basil, leaves picked
5 roasted tomato halves (page 92),
    chopped
½ cup roasted tomato juice (page 92)
1 recipe Basic Pasta Dough (page 165)
1 cup freshly grated Parmigiano-
    Reggiano

1. Wrap the ricotta in cheesecloth and place it in a strainer set over a bowl to drain for at least 45 minutes.

Here roasted tomatoes are added to zucchini and eggplant to make a ratatouille-like stuffing for lasagne.

2. Cut the onion, zucchini, eggplant, and pepper into strips about 1½ inches long and about ⅓ inch wide.

3. Heat 2 tablespoons of the oil in a large skillet over medium heat until the oil moves easily across the pan. Add the onion and the garlic and cook, stirring frequently, until the onion begins to soften, about 5 minutes. Add the pepper strips, cook for 1 or 2 minutes, then add the zucchini and eggplant. Add salt, pepper, and the bay leaf and cook, stirring frequently, until the peppers, zucchini, and eggplant soften, about 5 minutes.

4. Add the basil, roasted tomatoes, and 2 or 3 tablespoons of the roasted tomato juice. Cook, stirring occasionally, until all the vegetables are tender, about 5 minutes more, then set the mixture aside to cool. Remove and discard the bay leaf.

5. Heat the oven to 350°F. Divide the pasta dough in half. Roll out the first half in a pasta machine. Work from the largest setting to the smallest, rolling the dough through each setting twice, and stopping short of the final setting. Lay out the rolled sheet of dough on a clean work surface. Cut the dough into 10 pieces 6 to 7 inches long and about 2½ inches wide. Repeat with the remaining pasta

dough, rolling and cutting 10 additional pieces. Lay the cut pasta out on a clean work surface and allow it to dry for 5 to 10 minutes.

6. Bring a large pot of salted water to a boil over high heat. Add the cut pasta to the water one piece at a time. Cook the pasta just until it floats to the surface, then drain and rinse under cold water. Lay 5 sheets of warm pasta out on a clean work surface and sprinkle with 1 to 2 tablespoons of the Parmigiano-Reggiano (the cheese adheres to and is absorbed by the warm pasta). Reserve this pasta for the top layer of the lasagne.

7. Brush a medium baking dish with oil. Line the baking dish with a little over half the plain pasta, allowing about 2 inches of excess to drape over the sides (it is okay if the pasta overlaps). Cover the pasta with about half of the vegetable mixture, dot with half the ricotta, and sprinkle with about one-third of the remaining Parmigiano-Reggiano. Trim the remaining pieces of pasta so they fit the baking dish and lay them over the filling. Top the lasagne with the remaining vegetable mixture, remaining ricotta, and another third of the Parmigiano-Reggiano. Trim the reserved cheese-dusted pasta to fit the pan exactly, lay them over the filling, then fold the draped edges of the bottom layer over to seal.

8. Sprinkle the top with the rest of the Parmigiano-Reggiano, drizzle with the remaining 2 tablespoons of olive oil, and bake for 25 minutes. Spoon the remaining 5 or 6 tablespoons of roasted tomato juice over the lasagne and continue baking until the lasagne is golden and bubbly, about 20 minutes more. Allow the lasagne to rest for about 10 minutes, then cut and serve.

HEIRLOOM TOMATOES

Hundreds of years ago there were countless varieties of tomatoes that ranged wildly in size, shape, and color—from the palest white-green to deep eggplant purple. Over the years, science has worked to breed sturdy, uniform tomatoes that turn red before they are fully ripe, driving the original strains close to extinction. Unfortunately, this has been at the expense of flavor. In recent years, as consumers have learned the difference between vegetables that are mass-produced and those carefully grown on small farms, farmers have labored to bring back old strains like Brandywine, Tiger Stripe, Yellow Nugget, and John Gold onto the market. Whenever possible, try to buy your tomatoes at a farmstand or a market that specializes in good produce, and don't be afraid of variations in color, size, shape, and markings. When tomatoes are at their peak, do as I do; slice them, then drizzle with extra virgin olive oil, sea salt, and freshly ground pepper. Enjoy.

roasted tomato risotto

2 tablespoons olive oil
1 onion, peeled and diced
1½ cups Arborio or other short-grain
    rice
Kosher salt and freshly ground black
    pepper
6 to 8 cups White Chicken Stock (page
    69), warmed

3 roasted tomato halves (page 92),
    chopped
4 roasted garlic cloves (page 92), peeled
    and chopped
1 tablespoon unsalted butter
¼ cup freshly grated Parmigiano-
    Reggiano

1. Heat the oil in a medium saucepan over medium heat until it slides easily across the pan. Add the onion and cook, stirring occasionally, until soft, about 15 minutes. Add the rice, salt, and pepper and cook, stirring, until the rice is heated through and slightly translucent, about 1 minute.

In this recipe the roasted tomatoes and garlic cloves are added to a classic risotto.

2. Add enough stock to almost cover the rice, about 2 cups. Simmer, stirring frequently, until the rice has absorbed the stock, 5 to 10 minutes. Stir in the tomatoes, garlic, and another cup of stock. Cook, stirring, until the rice looks dry, then add another cup of stock. Continue gradually adding the stock, cooking, and stirring, until the rice is tender and creamy, about 25 minutes. Stir in the butter and cheese, season with salt and pepper, and serve.

clam ragout with pancetta, roasted tomatoes, and mustard greens

Shellfish with bacon is a classic combination. The sensation of salty, briny clams with slightly sweet pancetta is one of my favorites. This dish is good served with hearty bread, or over linguine. Substitute arugula if you can't find mustard greens.

6 ounces pancetta (or other unsmoked bacon), cut into strips about ½ inch thick and 2 inches long

2 garlic cloves, peeled and thinly sliced

1 shallot, peeled and thinly sliced

4 roasted tomato halves (page 92), coarsely chopped

¼ cup dry white wine

3 dozen Manila or littleneck clams, scrubbed and rinsed

4 cups mustard greens

3 or 4 tablespoons extra-virgin olive oil

1. Place the pancetta in a pot large enough to hold the clams. Cook over medium-low heat, stirring occasionally, until the pancetta is crisp, about 15 minutes. Remove the pancetta with a slotted spoon and drain on a plate lined with paper towels.

In this dish the roasted tomatoes are added to clams and bacon to create a hearty, rustic stew.

2. Discard all but about 2 tablespoons of fat. Increase the heat to medium and add the garlic and shallot. Cook, stirring occasionally, until fragrant, about 2 minutes, then add the roasted tomatoes. Cook about 1 minute. Add the wine and allow it to reduce until the pan is almost dry, about 3 minutes.

3. Add the clams and ¼ cup water. Cover and cook, stirring occasionally, until the clams open, about 10 minutes. Remove the lid and stir in the greens. Cook just until the greens are wilted, about 3 minutes. Divide the clams, greens, and broth among 4 shallow bowls. Top with pancetta, drizzle with olive oil, and serve.

sea bass stuffed with roasted tomatoes

Stuffing roasted tomatoes in between sea bass fillets helps to infuse their flavor into the fish. Once the whole thing is bundled, season it on both sides and cook it like a single piece of fish. Cut the string off with scissors before serving.

FOR THE FISH
4 (6-ounce) sea bass fillets, skin on
4 roasted tomato halves (page 92)
8 bay leaves
8 sprigs of fresh thyme
Kosher salt and freshly ground black
    pepper
2 to 3 tablespoons olive oil

FOR THE SAUCE
1½ cups roasted tomato juice (page 92)
3 tablespoons unsalted butter

1. **Preparing the fish.** Place 2 fillets on a clean cutting board, skin-side down. Arrange the other fillets on top of them, skin-side up. Cut each fish bundle into 2 equal pieces (you should have 4 small bundles). Lift the top fillets and place a roasted tomato half, bay leaf, and thyme sprig on each bottom fillet. Season with salt and pepper, then re-cover. Place a bay leaf and a thyme sprig on top of each bundle, then tie each bundle together with 2 or 3 pieces of kitchen string.

Here we tie roasted tomatoes between two sea bass fillets, and then pan roast. The tomato liquid is warmed and spooned over to make a simple sauce for the dish.

2. Heat the oil in a large skillet over medium-high heat until it shimmers. Season the fish with salt and pepper and cook, bay-leaf-side down, until the skin crisps, about 5 minutes. Turn the fish, reduce the heat to medium-low, and continue cooking until the second side is crisp and the fish flakes easily, about 5 minutes more (thicker pieces will take a bit longer).

3. **Making the sauce and assembling the dish.** Warm the roasted tomato juice in a saucepan over low heat. Gradually whisk in the butter. Spoon the sauce onto 4 warm plates, place a fish bundle on each plate, and serve.

seared tuna with roasted tomato vinaigrette and fennel salad

SERVES 4

FOR THE VINAIGRETTE
2 roasted tomato halves (page 92)
¼ cup roasted tomato juice (page 92), warmed
2 tablespoons red wine vinegar
Kosher salt and freshly ground black pepper
½ cup extra-virgin olive oil

FOR THE SALAD
1 small fennel bulb, cored and very thinly sliced
½ cup mixed fresh herb leaves (such as tarragon, basil, chervil, dill, and parsley)

1 tablespoon extra-virgin olive oil
Kosher salt and freshly ground black pepper

FOR THE TUNA
2 tablespoons extra-virgin olive oil
1½ pounds tuna cut into 4 1-inch-thick steaks
Kosher salt and freshly ground black pepper
4 roasted tomato halves

1. Making the vinaigrette. Combine 2 roasted tomato halves, the tomato juice, vinegar, salt, and pepper in a blender or food processor and purée. With the machine running, slowly add the olive oil and process until emulsified, then set aside.

In this recipe the roasted tomatoes are used in two different ways: First, they are used to make a vinaigrette, then they are placed on the plate as a bed for the tuna.

2. Making the salad. Combine the fennel and herbs in a small bowl. Dress with 1 tablespoon of olive oil, salt, and pepper and mix well.

3. Cooking the tuna and assembling the dish. Heat a large heavy skillet over medium-high heat. Add the oil. Season the tuna on both sides with salt and pepper and sear (about 2 minutes per side for rare). Transfer the tuna to a cutting board and slice thin across the grain. To serve, arrange the remaining roasted tomato halves on plates. Place the tuna slices over the tomatoes, top with fennel salad, and drizzle with tomato vinaigrette.

braised lamb shanks with roasted tomato

SERVES 4

2 to 3 tablespoons peanut oil
Kosher salt and freshly ground black
    pepper
4 lamb shanks
1 onion, peeled and coarsely chopped
1 leek, white part only, trimmed and
    coarsely chopped
1 carrot, peeled and coarsely chopped
1 celery stalk, coarsely chopped
3 garlic cloves, peeled and chopped

1 to 2 tablespoons tomato paste
1 bunch of fresh tarragon, leaves picked
About 10 cups Brown Chicken Stock
    (page 70)
8 roasted tomato halves (page 92)
8 roasted garlic cloves (page 92), peeled
5 cups cooked cannellini beans (page
    260), drained
4 cups arugula

1. Heat the oven to 325° F. Heat the oil in a large, deep oven-proof skillet or roasting pan over medium-high heat. Salt and pepper the shanks, then, working in batches, brown them on all sides, about 25 minutes per batch. Transfer the shanks to a plate, reduce the heat to medium, and add the onion, leek, carrot, celery, and garlic. Cook, stirring occasionally, until the vegetables begin to soften, about 10 minutes. Add the tomato paste and cook, stirring, until the vegetables are well coated, about 2 minutes more.

The roasted tomatoes are especially versatile here. They add richness and complexity to braised lamb shanks, and the braising liquid makes an intense broth in which to serve the lamb and the beans.

2. Return the shanks to the skillet. Add half the tarragon and enough stock to surround the shanks (about 10 cups). Bring the stock to a simmer. Partially cover the pan, and transfer it to the oven. Cook the shanks (the braising liquid should barely bubble) until the meat pulls easily from the bone, 2 to 3 hours.

3. Transfer the shanks to a plate. Strain the braising liquid and discard the solids. Return the liquid to the skillet and bring it to a simmer over medium heat. Skim.

4. Return the shanks to the liquid. Add the tomatoes and garlic. Simmer over medium heat, basting occasionally, until the broth has reduced by one-third, about 20 minutes. Add the beans, arugula, and remaining tarragon and cook until the arugula is just wilted, 3 minutes. Spoon into 4 large bowls and serve.

caramelized tomato tarts

SERVES 4

This is a twist on the classic apple tarte Tatin, using roasted tomatoes in place of apples. To cut down on the sweetness of the dish, we add sherry vinegar to the caramelized sugar. The tart is great on its own or can be served as a garnish for roasted lamb.

4 tablespoons sugar
¼ teaspoon sherry vinegar
4 roasted garlic cloves (page 92)
12 Niçoise olives, pitted
4 roasted tomato halves (page 92)
Kosher salt and freshly ground black
    pepper

1 to 1½ cups (a half recipe) Onion
    Confit (see page 235)
8 ounces prepared puff pastry (defrosted
    if frozen)

1. Heat the oven to 425°F. Combine the sugar with 1 tablespoon of water in a small saucepan and heat over medium heat. Swirl the pan until the sugar has completely dissolved, then let the mixture boil, swirling occasionally, until the resulting caramel is nut brown. Remove the saucepan from the heat. Add the sherry vinegar to the caramel, swirling the pan until thoroughly combined.

2. Pour the caramel into four 4-ounce ramekins. Allow the caramel to cool for a minute or so, then place 1 garlic clove, 3 olives, and a tomato half into each ramekin. Add salt and pepper and top with onion confit.

3. Cut the puff pastry into circles slightly larger than the opening of the ramekins (these will become the tart crusts). Place the pastry circles over the onion confit, then transfer the ramekins to a baking sheet and bake until the pastry is puffed and golden, about 20 minutes. Allow the tarts to cool for 1 to 2 minutes, then carefully turn them out onto plates. Serve warm or at room temperature.

mushrooms

WHEN I WAS SMALL, MY GRANDFATHER WORKED FOR Public Service Electric & Gas, installing power lines in rural New Jersey. It was hard, physical work, but somehow my grandfather always found time to walk into the woods and pick some wild mushrooms for his dinner. At home, he would toss a penny and a nickel with the mushrooms into a pot of boiling water. If the coins changed color, the mushrooms were poisonous, or so he said. I have no idea whether this works or if Grandpa simply had luck on his side. He's no longer with us, but it wasn't the mushrooms that did him in.

These days there are plenty of good cultivated varieties available, such as portobello, shiitake, and hen-of-the-woods. I prefer the flavor of the wild varieties—rich, earthy morels; the slightly piney quality of chanterelles; and the king of all mushrooms, the cèpes, or porcini. When mushrooms are this good, it's important to cook them the right way.

I think of my grandfather every time I eat wild mushrooms.

For some reason, when young cooks first come into my kitchen, they all seem to cook mushrooms the wrong way; they throw the entire batch into a very hot pan, crowding them together. Immediately, the mushrooms release water, the temperature in the pan drops, the water pools in the pan without evaporating, and the mushrooms stew in the liquid and become a watery, rubbery mess. Instead, the mushrooms should be cooked in small batches, which will keep the temperature in the pan from dropping and will give them sufficient

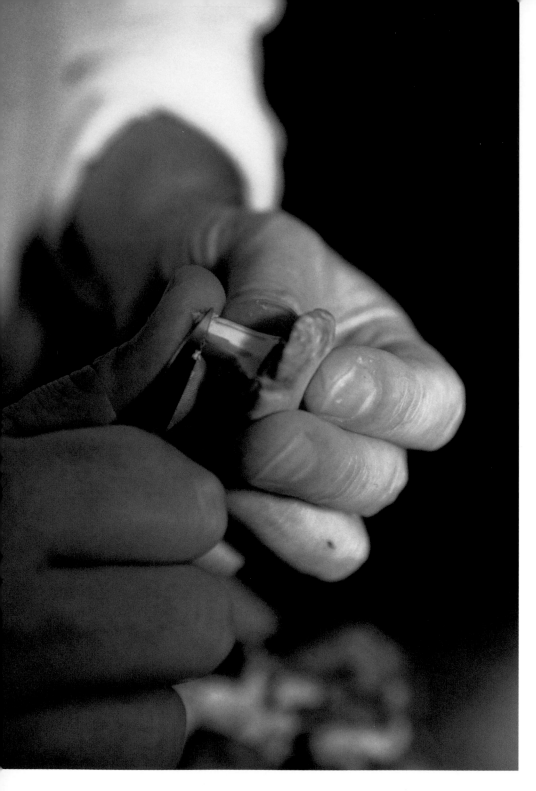

space for their water to be released as steam. They should not be moved around much, since this only bunches them further and keeps the mushrooms from caramelizing and developing their deep, nutty flavors.

basic mushroom technique

1. Heat a small amount of olive oil in a pan. Add a small batch of mushrooms. After a few moments they will start to release moisture, which should evaporate quickly. Avoid moving the mushrooms around excessively.

2. When the mushrooms start to brown, add a small amount of butter to the pan. Gently toss the mushrooms in the butter.

3. Once the mushrooms have browned sufficiently, remove to a paper towel and start on the next batch.

a few tips on choosing, storing, and cleaning mushrooms

Once harvested, mushrooms immediately start to lose moisture, starch, and sugars, so look for the freshest you can find, and try to buy whole mushrooms, not diced or cut. They should still feel moist and relatively heavy for their size: Dry, hollow-feeling mushrooms have already started to break down. If you are buying wild mushrooms, turn them over: If you see small pinholes in the mushrooms, don't buy them, as worms may have gotten to them first. Place mushrooms in a paper bag and refrigerate if you don't intend to use them right away.

Mushrooms need to be cleaned, but I don't recommend rinsing them because it washes away some of the flavor. Instead, start by trimming away the dry tip of the stem, and then scrape the stem clean with a small paring knife. You can scrape the top of the mushroom in the same way, or wipe it off with a damp paper towel or soft toothbrush. If you feel the need to rinse them, drop your mushrooms into *standing* water, not running, then lift them out of the water with your hands, and blot dry on paper towels.

pan-roasted mushrooms

SERVES 4 AS A FIRST COURSE OR SIDE DISH

I call these mushrooms pan-roasted, because they are cut on the thick side and cooked more slowly than a traditional quick sauté, for optimal flavor.

4 to 6 tablespoons extra-virgin olive oil
2 pounds mixed wild and cultivated
    mushrooms, cleaned, trimmed, and
    thickly sliced
Kosher salt and freshly ground black
    pepper
1 or 2 shallots, peeled and finely
    chopped

2 garlic cloves, peeled and finely
    chopped
2 tablespoons unsalted butter
2 tablespoons fresh thyme leaves
2 tablespoons chopped fresh tarragon
    (optional)

1. Heat about 1 tablespoon of the oil in a large, heavy skillet over medium-high heat until it shimmers. Add just enough mushrooms to loosely cover the bottom of the skillet (you should be able to see the pan between the mushrooms). Season the mushrooms with salt and pepper. Cook for about 2 minutes, then gently turn the mushrooms over as they brown and soften.

These pan-roasted mushrooms are the "ingredient" upon which the following recipes build.

2. Add a little chopped shallot and garlic, some butter, and some thyme and tarragon. Continue cooking the mushrooms until they are tender, about 2 minutes more, then transfer them to a paper towel. Wipe out the skillet and repeat the process, cooking the mushrooms in small batches.

3. Just before serving, add a bit more butter or oil to the skillet and warm the mushrooms over medium heat. Season with salt and pepper and serve.

Roasted Sea Scallops with Mushrooms (see page 112).

roasted sea scallops with mushrooms

SERVES 4

To make this dish, you can prepare the pan-roasted mushrooms up to one hour ahead; reheat them once the scallops are plated.

8 to 12 large sea scallops, depending upon the size, muscle removed
Kosher salt and freshly ground black pepper
2 tablespoons peanut oil

3 tablespoons unsalted butter
1 recipe Pan-Roasted Mushrooms (page 110)
2 tablespoons fresh thyme leaves
1 teaspoon chopped fresh tarragon

1. Dry the scallops thoroughly with paper towels, then season on both sides with salt and pepper. Heat the oil in a large, well-seasoned skillet over medium-high heat until it shimmers. Add the scallops and adjust the heat so the oil sizzles but doesn't smoke. Cook the scallops until they begin to brown, about 2 minutes, then turn them and add 1 tablespoon of the butter. Cook the scallops, basting them with butter, until they are opaque and beginning to firm, about 1 minute more. Arrange them on serving plates.

In this dish the mushrooms and the scallops are roasted side by side. The mushrooms lend an earthiness to the sweet flavor of the scallops.

2. Melt the remaining 2 tablespoons of butter in the skillet over medium heat. Add the mushrooms, thyme, and tarragon and warm, stirring gently, just until the mushrooms are heated through. Spoon the mushrooms around the scallops and serve.

marinated mushrooms

¼ cup plus 2 tablespoons extra-virgin
   olive oil
2 leeks, white part only, trimmed, halved
   lengthwise, and thinly sliced
1 small onion, peeled, quartered lengthwise, and thinly sliced
1 carrot, peeled and thinly sliced
2 celery stalks, peeled and thinly sliced
Kosher salt
1 garlic clove, peeled

1 bay leaf
1 tablespoon coriander seeds
1 recipe Pan-Roasted Mushrooms
   (page 110) prepared without the
   optional tarragon
Freshly ground black pepper
2½ tablespoons sherry vinegar
¼ cup Brown Chicken Stock (page 70)
2 sprigs of fresh thyme
2 sprigs of fresh flat-leaf parsley

1. Heat 2 tablespoons of the oil in a large skillet over medium-low heat until it slides easily across the pan. Add the sliced leeks, onion, carrot, and celery. Season with salt and cook, stirring occasionally, until the vegetables begin to soften, about 10 minutes. Add the garlic, bay leaf, and coriander seeds and continue cooking until the vegetables are very tender, 10 to 15 minutes more.

This recipe begins with the pan-roasted mushrooms (page 110), which are marinated in a combination of chicken stock, vinegar, and aromatic vegetables. Reserve the liquid from the marinade for braising salmon, page 115.

2. Add the mushrooms to the skillet and season liberally with black pepper. Add the vinegar, let it bubble for a second or two, then add the chicken stock, thyme, and parsley. Simmer for 1 to 2 minutes, then remove the skillet from the heat. Add the remaining ¼ cup of olive oil and set aside, allowing the mushrooms to cool slowly in the marinade. Cover and refrigerate for at least 2 hours before serving.

salmon braised with mushrooms

Just as fatty cuts of meat are best for braising, the higher fat content in salmon makes it a good choice for this dish. Unlike meat, though, the salmon does not need to be cooked for hours to achieve tenderness. Try to buy the thickest salmon fillets available for this dish and braise until just cooked through.

2 tablespoons extra-virgin olive oil
4 (6-ounce) center-cut salmon fillets, about 1½ inches thick
Kosher salt and freshly ground black pepper

1 cup Brown Chicken Stock (page 70)
1 recipe Marinated Mushrooms (page 113)
1 tablespoon unsalted butter

1. Heat the oil in a large skillet over medium-high heat until it shimmers. Season the salmon with salt and pepper on both wider (cut) sides. Add the pieces to the skillet, with the seasoned side down. Adjust the heat so the oil sizzles but does not smoke. Cook for about 3 minutes without turning (the cooked side will be golden), then transfer the salmon to a plate. Wipe out the skillet.

Here the salmon is braised in the liquid from the marinated mushrooms.

2. Add the chicken stock and marinated mushrooms to the skillet and bring to a simmer over medium heat. Nestle the salmon, cooked-side up, among the mushrooms. Gently simmer, basting frequently, until the salmon is cooked, 2 to 4 minutes for medium rare.

3. Transfer the salmon to serving plates. Stir the butter, salt, and pepper into the mushrooms. Spoon mushrooms onto each plate and serve.

polenta gratin with mushroom "bolognese"

Bolognese usually refers to a rustic meat sauce. This version uses wild mushrooms in place of the veal found in the classic dish. When buying polenta, do not buy the precooked variety, which is cooked, dried, and ground fine. The uncooked variety takes longer, but the flavor and texture are much better.

FOR THE BOLOGNESE
2 tablespoons peanut oil
1 onion, peeled and diced
1 carrot, peeled and diced
1 celery stalk, peeled and diced
Kosher salt and freshly ground black
    pepper
1 garlic clove, peeled and minced
½ to ¾ pound mixed wild and cultivated
    mushrooms, cleaned, trimmed, and
    diced

1 tablespoon fresh thyme leaves
1 tomato, seeded and diced
1 cup Brown Chicken Stock (page 70)

FOR THE POLENTA
1 cup polenta
Kosher salt
¼ cup extra-virgin olive oil

3 or 4 tablespoons freshly grated
    Parmigiano-Reggiano

1. Preparing the Bolognese sauce. Heat the peanut oil in a large skillet over medium heat until it moves easily across the pan. Add the onion, carrot, celery, salt, and pepper and cook, stirring occasionally, until the vegetables begin to soften, about 5 minutes. Add the garlic, cook for 1 minute, then add the mushrooms and thyme leaves. Cook, stirring frequently, until the mushrooms are almost tender, about 3 minutes. Add the tomato, cook for about 2 minutes more, then add the stock 2 tablespoons at a time, bringing the pan to a simmer before each addition. Simmer the Bolognese until it is concentrated but not yet dry, about 30 minutes. Set aside to cool.

In this dish we add stock and aromatic vegetables to pan-roasted mushrooms to make a rich, meatless sauce for polenta.

2. Making the polenta. Moisten the polenta with 2 tablespoons of water, mixing well with your hands. Bring 4 cups of water to a boil in a saucepan over high heat. Add a pinch of salt and gradually stir in the polenta. Stirring constantly, bring the

polenta to a boil, then reduce the heat to low. Cook the polenta, stirring occasionally, until it is no longer grainy, about 30 minutes. Stir the olive oil into the polenta, season with salt, and remove it from the heat.

3. Assembling the gratin. Heat the oven to 350° F. Spoon half the polenta into a medium baking dish and cover with half of the sauce. Spoon in the remaining polenta, spread it evenly, then sprinkle with the Parmigiano-Reggiano. Transfer the remaining sauce to a small saucepan and reserve.

4. Bake the gratin until the top is golden, about 40 minutes. Just before serving, warm the reserved sauce over low heat. Divide the gratin and sauce among 4 plates and serve.

pan-roasted quail with swiss chard and mushrooms

SERVES 4

Quail is a red-meat bird, best cooked and served on the rare side. The golden raisins add a sweet counterpoint to the earthy chard and the mushrooms.

½ cup golden raisins
1½ pounds young Swiss chard (about 2 bunches)
Kosher salt
4 tablespoons peanut oil
Freshly ground black pepper
4 quail, quartered

¾ to 1 pound mixed wild and cultivated mushrooms, cleaned, trimmed, and thickly sliced
8 spring onions or scallions, trimmed and white part halved lengthwise
1 to 2 tablespoons unsalted butter
1 to 2 tablespoons Brown Chicken Stock (page 70)

1. Place the raisins in a small bowl, cover them with very hot water, and set aside for at least 30 minutes to plump, replacing the hot water once or twice. Drain the raisins and set aside.

The ingredients in this recipe are roasted separately, then together, flavoring each other and acquiring glazed flavors with the addition of brown chicken stock.

2. Meanwhile, separate the chard leaves and stems. Peel the stems and cut them into thin lengths, about 3 inches long. Bring a large pot of salted water to a boil over high heat. Blanch the leaves in the water until bright green, about 1 minute. Drain them, rinse under cold water, squeeze thoroughly, coarsely chop, and set aside.

3. Heat 1 tablespoon of the oil in a large skillet over medium heat until it moves easily across the pan. Salt and pepper the quail, then brown the breasts, skin-side down, for about 4 minutes. Turn the breasts, cook 1 minute more, then transfer to a plate. Brown the legs, 3 to 4 minutes per side. Set them aside with the breasts.

4. Wipe out the skillet. Heat another tablespoon of the oil over medium-high heat until it shimmers. Add the mushrooms and cook for about 2 minutes, then gently

turn the mushrooms over as they brown. Cook for 1 minute more, season with salt and pepper and remove to a plate. (The mushrooms will be nicely browned but not yet tender.)

5. Add the remaining 2 tablespoons of oil to the skillet. Cook the onions and the chard stems over medium heat until they begin to soften, 1 to 2 minutes. Add salt and pepper and cook for 1 to 2 minutes more, then add the quail legs. Cook, turning the legs occasionally, for about 5 minutes, then add the breasts, mushrooms, and butter. Cook, turning the quail and mushrooms in the melting butter for about 2 minutes. Add the raisins, and begin to deglaze the pan with the stock, adding it a teaspoon at a time and waiting until the pan is almost (but not quite) dry before adding more. Continue to turn the quail and vegetables in the sauce. When all the stock has been added and the juices from the quail run clear, about 5 minutes more, add the chard leaves. Cook for 1 to 2 minutes longer, then serve.

caramelized mushroom tarts

I came up with this dish as a hearty final course for Gramercy Tavern's vegetable tasting menu. The Caramelized Tomato Tarts (page 105) from summer had been so popular that we expanded the idea to mushrooms, starting with a large single cèpe, cut in half, laid over onion confit in a tart shell. After cèpe season was over, I began experimenting with different varieties of wild mushroom, all of which work well.

2 large shallots
3 to 4 tablespoons extra-virgin olive oil
¾ pound mixed wild and cultivated
    mushrooms, cleaned, trimmed, and
    thickly sliced
Kosher salt and freshly ground pepper
1 garlic clove, peeled and minced

1 tablespoon fresh thyme leaves
4 tablespoons sugar
¼ teaspoon sherry vinegar
1 to 1½ cups (a half recipe) Onion
    Confit (page 235)
8 ounces prepared puff pastry (defrosted
    if frozen)

1. Heat the oven to 375° F. Wrap 1 shallot in aluminum foil and bake it until it is soft, about 15 minutes. Remove the roasted shallot from the oven, let it cool slightly, then peel it and set aside. Peel and mince the remaining shallot.

2. Heat 1 to 2 tablespoons of the oil in a heavy skillet over medium-high heat until it shimmers. Add just enough mushrooms to cover the bottom of the pan in a single layer. Add salt and pepper and cook, turning the mushrooms when they begin to brown, about 2 minutes. Add some minced shallot, garlic, and thyme and continue cooking until the mushrooms are tender, about 2 minutes more. Transfer the sautéed mushrooms to a plate, wipe out the skillet, and repeat, cooking the remaining mushrooms in batches.

3. Increase the oven temperature to 425° F. Combine the sugar and 1 tablespoon water in a small saucepan over medium heat. Swirl the pan until the sugar has completely dissolved, then let the mixture boil, swirling occasionally, until the sugar caramelizes and turns nut brown. Swirl the sherry vinegar into the caramel, then remove it from the heat.

4. Pour the caramel into four 4-ounce ramekins and allow it to cool for about a minute. Cut the roasted shallot into 4 pieces. Place a piece of shallot in each ramekin, cover with sautéed mushrooms, and top with Onion Confit.

5. Cut the puff pastry into circles slightly larger than the opening of the ramekins (these will become the tart crusts). Lay the pastry circles over the Onion Confit and place the ramekins on a baking sheet. Bake the tarts until the pastry is puffed and golden, about 20 minutes. Cool for a minute or so, then carefully unmold onto plates and serve warm or at room temperature.

ON SALT

I was around ten years old the day I discovered salt. It was a late summer afternoon, just cooling into evening, at my family's swim club. My father had brought along some club steaks to grill later for the family, but I was too hungry to wait, so I tossed one on the grill for myself, pulling it off when it seemed done. I started to wolf down the meat when I realized something—with a jolt of surprise—that had never occurred to me before. It needed salt. Up until now my food had been cooked (and seasoned) for me, so this was an altogether new thought. I added a little salt and took another bite. I remember being literally blown away by the difference it made. The steak was so good, I grilled another one, then and there, and then a third, salting them and eating them right where I stood. I started to play with the idea, adding a little more salt at a time and tasting the difference that made—the point at which the steak went from being flavorful, to too salty. I was focused completely, cooking and salting and eating as I went. Suddenly there was an angry chorus of grown-up voices around me. The steaks for the whole family were gone.

What I discovered that day is that salt does far more than add saltiness to a dish. It interacts with the flavors of the ingredients and your taste buds, "waking" up everything along the way. This is especially noticeable in a dish that is both sweet and sour, like Green Tomato Chutney (page 224) or Corn Relish (page 213). I urge you to follow one of these recipes and then taste the completed dish. Then add only a grain or two of salt and taste again. As you continue to do this, you'll notice that the sweet flavors become sweeter, the acids become brighter; all the flavors in the dish become more vibrant. I like to walk my new cooks through this—tasting a finished dish, while adding salt a grain at a time—so they can learn the power of salt for themselves.

braised artichokes

It may have choked Artie, but it ain't gonna choke Stymie.
—Stymie, Our Gang

gROWING UP, I KNEW ONLY ONE WAY TO EAT AN ARTICHOKE: boiled, the leaves pulled off and dipped into melted butter. Although it was delicious, I later learned that this barely skims the surface of what an artichoke can be or do. The real prize of the artichoke is the heart, nestled beneath the leaves, above the stem and choke. Artichokes are both woodsy and delicate, with a flavor that is equal parts sweet root vegetable and grassy shoot. The big problem for people seems to be learning how to "clean" an artichoke, or access the heart. For that reason I've included the instructions here, with pictures, on page 130. The braised artichoke recipe that follows is actually derived from an old Provençal dish, Artichokes Barigoule. I love to prepare a large batch and keep it in the fridge, where it keeps for about two weeks, using it in a variety of ways, as I've shown.

artichokes braised in olive oil and white wine

SERVES 4 AS AN APPETIZER

This recipe is the cornerstone for all of the recipes that follow in this section. Be sure to use a pot large enough to hold the artichokes in a single layer.

3 lemons
8 large artichokes
1 medium yellow onion, peeled
2 small leeks, tops trimmed and green outer leaves discarded
2 celery stalks, trimmed and peeled
2 small carrots, peeled
2 slices bacon (optional)

½ cup extra-virgin olive oil
Kosher salt
4 garlic cloves, peeled
Freshly ground black pepper
2 bay leaves
4 sprigs of fresh tarragon
4 sprigs of fresh thyme
1¾ cups dry white wine

1. Combine the juice of 2½ of the lemons and 2 quarts of water in a large bowl. Trim each artichoke, removing the stem, leaves, and choke and rubbing from time to time with the remaining half lemon. (See page 130 for detailed instructions.) Set the trimmed artichoke bottoms aside in the lemon water.

This dish can also be made with cauliflower, endive, fennel, or white asparagus in place of artichokes. Stick to white vegetables, however, as green vegetables will turn brown.

2. Cut the onion lengthwise, then slice thin. Quarter the leeks lengthwise, then cut them into thin strips about 2 inches long. Thinly slice the celery and carrots. (You will have roughly equal amounts of onion, leeks, and celery.)

3. If you are using the bacon, render it for 2 to 3 minutes, then add ¼ cup of the oil, otherwise just heat the oil in a large high-sided pot over medium heat until it slides easily across the pan. Add the onion, leeks, celery, and carrots—the aromatic vegetables—to the pot. Season with salt, then reduce the heat to medium-low and slowly cook the aromatic vegetables, stirring occasionally, until they are tender but not brown, about 20 minutes. Add the garlic and cook for another minute.

4. Drain the artichokes and add them to the pot. Add a little more salt and pepper, enough olive oil to coat the artichokes (about 2 tablespoons), the bay leaves,

and half the tarragon and thyme. Mix gently and arrange the artichokes in a single layer. Pour in the wine and enough water to cover the artichokes, about 2 cups, and bring to a simmer. Partially cover the pot, reduce the heat, and gently simmer until the artichokes can be easily pierced with a knife, about 30 minutes.

5. Coarsely chop the remaining tarragon and thyme. Add the herbs to the artichokes and remove the pot from the heat. Allow the artichokes to cool slowly in the braising liquid, then garnish with the aromatic vegetables and some additional herbs. Serve at room temperature, chilled as a cold dish, or heated through.

1. Trim the stem, leaving about 1 inch. Break off the tough outer leaves.

2. Lay the artichoke on its side and chop off the tops of the inner leaves, about 1½ inches from the stem.

3. Use a paring knife to peel away the outer layers that surround the heart, as though peeling an apple.

4. Use a spoon to scrape out the immature leaves and the fuzzy choke.

5. Trim the top of the heart. Rub with lemon to keep the artichoke from discoloring.

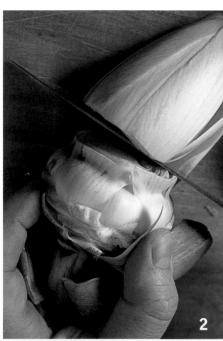

artichoke salad

5 braised artichokes (page 129), thickly sliced

2 cups arugula, trimmed (about 2 bunches)

1½ tablespoons chopped Lemon Confit (page 258)

Kosher salt and freshly ground black pepper

2 tablespoons extra-virgin olive oil

2 baby artichokes

¼ pound piece Parmigiano-Reggiano

1. Combine the braised artichokes, arugula, and ½ tablespoon of the Lemon Confit in a large bowl. Add salt and pepper and 1 tablespoon of the oil. Divide the salad among 4 plates.

In this recipe we pair the braised artichokes with thinly sliced raw artichokes to form a salad.

2. Trim the baby artichokes, cutting off the leaf ends and stem, then pulling away the tough outer leaves. Slice the artichokes as thin as possible, then dress immediately with the remaining Lemon Confit and olive oil. Arrange the sliced artichokes over the salad, top with shaved Parmigiano-Reggiano, and serve.

artichoke vinaigrette

½ cup artichoke braising liquid with aromatic vegetables (page 129)

1 egg yolk

1 tablespoon white wine vinegar

1 tablespoon fresh lemon juice

1 braised artichoke (page 129)

Kosher salt and freshly ground black pepper

¼ cup extra-virgin olive oil

¼ cup peanut oil

Combine the braising liquid and aromatic vegetables, egg yolk, vinegar, lemon juice, and artichoke in a blender. Add a pinch each of salt and pepper and purée. With the motor running, gradually add the olive and peanut oils. Thin, if necessary, with additional braising liquid.

Here we purée a small amount of the artichokes with some of their braising liquid and vinegar to make a vinaigrette. It is delicious as a dressing for salads or as a light sauce for roasted fish.

orecchiette with artichokes, cabbage, and cranberry beans

SERVES 4

FOR THE BEANS
2 tablespoons extra-virgin olive oil
½ small yellow onion, peeled
1 small leek, white part trimmed and cut
    in half lengthwise
1 small celery stalk, peeled, trimmed,
    and cut in half
1 small carrot, peeled, trimmed, and cut
    in half
Kosher salt
1 sprig of fresh thyme
1 garlic clove, peeled and crushed
¾ cup dried cranberry beans (or 1 cup
    shelled fresh beans, about 1 pound
    unshelled)

FOR THE RAGOUT
½ small head Savoy cabbage
Kosher salt
½ bunch scallions, white part trimmed,
    halved, then cut into 2- to 3-inch
    lengths
4 braised artichokes (page 129), sliced
2 cups Brown Chicken Stock (page 70)
1 to 2 teaspoons fresh thyme leaves
Freshly ground black pepper
½ pound orecchiette
2 tablespoons unsalted butter
Shaved Parmigiano-Reggiano

1. **Cooking the beans.** Heat the oil in a large pot over medium heat until it slides easily across the pan. Add the onion, leek, celery, and carrot. Season with salt and cook, stirring occasionally, until the vegetables begin to soften, about 10 minutes. Add the thyme and garlic. Cook for another minute or so and then add the beans. Mix well and add water to cover (about 5 cups), season with salt, and slowly bring just to a simmer over medium-low heat. Cook the beans just below a simmer, skimming occasionally, until they are tender, 1 to 2 hours. Remove the beans from the heat and allow them to cool in the cooking liquid.

The artichokes in this dish are tossed with cabbage, beans, and pasta to make a hearty, flavorful ragout.

2. **Preparing the ragout.** Remove the core from the cabbage, separate the leaves, and cut out and throw away the tough central ribs. Tear or cut the leaves into large pieces.

3. Cook the cabbage in boiling salted water until it is tender, 3 to 5 minutes. Drain, then rinse under cold water.

4. Drain the beans and discard the flavoring herbs, onion, leek, celery, and carrot. Place the beans, cabbage, scallions, and artichoke hearts in a large saucepan. Add the stock and thyme leaves, season with salt and pepper, and bring to a simmer.

5. Assembling the dish. Bring a large pot of salted water to a boil over high heat. Add the pasta and cook, stirring occasionally, until al dente, about 8 minutes; drain. Add the butter and the pasta to the cabbage mixture. Add salt and pepper to taste and mix well. Serve topped with shaved Parmigiano-Reggiano.

artichoke ravioli with artichokes, peas, and asparagus

SERVES 4 AS A FIRST COURSE

FOR THE RAVIOLI

2 braised artichokes (page 129)

3 tablespoons braised aromatic
    vegetables, including 1 garlic clove
    (page 129), drained, liquid reserved

Kosher salt and freshly ground black
    pepper

1 recipe Basic Pasta Dough (page 165)

Coarse cornmeal

FOR THE ARTICHOKE RAGOUT

Kosher salt

1 cup shelled peas

1 cup asparagus tips (about 1 bunch)

1 cup Brown Chicken Stock (page 70)

¼ cup artichoke braising liquid
    (page 129)

2 tablespoons unsalted butter

4 braised artichokes (page 129),
    quartered

¼ cup mixed chopped fresh herbs such
    as chervil, chives, basil, or tarragon

Freshly ground black pepper

Extra-virgin olive oil

Shaved black truffle (optional)

1. **Preparing the ravioli filling.** Purée the artichokes with the garlic and braised vegetables, adding only enough braising liquid to smooth out the mixture. Add salt and pepper to taste and refrigerate until ready to use.

Here the artichokes are puréed and used as a stuffing for ravioli. A few more artichokes, sliced and tossed with asparagus, peas, and truffle, make a delicious garnish for the dish.

2. **Making the ravioli.** Divide the dough in half. Roll out the first half in a pasta machine. Working from the largest setting to the smallest, roll the dough through each setting twice, and stop short of the final setting. Lay the dough on a clean work surface. Using half the filling, place spoonfuls in two rows of three over half the pasta sheet (there should be about 2 inches between each spoonful). Brush the other half of the sheet lightly with water, then fold it over the first. Run your fingers around each pocket of filling, pressing to seal, then cut the ravioli into squares or rounds. Transfer to a baking sheet dusted with corn-

meal. Repeat with remaining dough and filling. Set aside for about 15 minutes to dry slightly, then turn them over and set aside for 15 minutes more.

3. **Making the ragout and assembling the dish.** Bring a large pot of salted water to a boil over high heat. Add the peas and cook until tender, about 3 minutes, remove with a slotted spoon, rinse under cold water, drain again, and set aside. Add the asparagus to the boiling water and cook until tender, about 3 minutes, then drain, rinse under cold water, drain again, and add to the peas. Refill the pot with salted water and bring to a boil over high heat. Add the ravioli and cook until tender, about 3 minutes. (The ravioli will float when done—but taste a corner to make sure.)

4. Meanwhile, bring the stock to a simmer in a large saucepan. Add the braising liquid and the butter, then the quartered artichokes, peas, and asparagus. Add the herbs and ravioli, season to taste with salt and pepper, heat through, and serve dressed with extra-virgin olive oil. Garnish with shaved black truffle.

quick-braised striped bass with artichokes and zucchini

SERVES 4

2 small, young zucchini, halved
    lengthwise, or 1 large zucchini,
    halved and seeded
Kosher salt
4 tomatoes, peeled
2 pounds sea bass fillet (skin on), cut
    into 4 pieces
Freshly ground black pepper

2 tablespoons peanut oil
1 cup artichoke braising liquid with
    aromatic vegetables (page 129)
4 braised artichokes (page 129), sliced
¼ cup chopped fresh flat-leaf parsley
Zest of 1 lemon, finely chopped
2 to 3 tablespoons extra-virgin olive oil

1. Slice the zucchini into thin semicircles and cook them in boiling salted water until tender, about 3 minutes. Rinse under cold water, drain well, and set aside.

2. Cut the tomatoes into quarters. Remove the seeds from the tomatoes, then cut the quarters into thin lengths. (You will have roughly equal amounts of zucchini and tomato.)

This recipe uses the liquid from the braised artichokes as a braising liquid for striped bass. The artichokes themselves are sliced and added to the pan to round out the dish.

3. Rinse the fish, pat it dry, and salt and pepper it on both sides. Heat the peanut oil in a large skillet over medium-high heat until it shimmers. Add the fish, skin-side down, and cook, working in batches if you need to. Continue cooking the fish without moving it, until the skin side is crisp (the edges will appear lightly browned), about 3 minutes, then transfer it to a plate.

4. Wipe out the skillet, add the braising liquid with aromatic vegetables, and bring to a simmer over medium heat. Add the zucchini, tomatoes, and artichokes and reduce the heat to medium-low. Lay the fish, skin-side up, over the vegetables and gently simmer, spooning the broth over the fish, until the fish flakes easily, about 4 minutes. Add the parsley and lemon zest to the broth, then transfer the fish to serving bowls. Add the olive oil to the broth and adjust the seasoning with salt and pepper. Spoon the broth and vegetables over the fish and serve.

slow-braised chicken with artichokes

SERVES 4

2 tablespoons peanut oil
Kosher salt and freshly ground black
    pepper
4 chicken legs
4 chicken thighs
1 large yellow onion, peeled and cut into
    8 pieces
3 carrots, peeled, each cut into about 4
    pieces
3 celery stalks, peeled, each cut into
    about 4 pieces

4 garlic cloves, peeled
4 sprigs of fresh thyme plus additional
    for garnish
4 sprigs of fresh tarragon plus additional
    for garnish
1¼ cups Brown Chicken Stock
    (page 70)
4 braised artichokes (page 129),
    quartered
2 tablespoons unsalted butter

1. Heat the oven to 350° F. Heat the oil in a large ovenproof skillet over medium-high heat until it shimmers. Salt and pepper the chicken on both sides, then, working in batches, brown the chicken, about 7 minutes per side. Transfer the chicken to a plate.

In this recipe artichokes are added at the end of the braise to flavor the basting liquid in the pan. The flavors of the chicken, artichokes, and aromatic vegetables are intended to come together to form an integrated whole.

2. Pour off all but enough fat to coat the skillet (about 2 tablespoons). Add the onion, carrots, celery, and a little salt. Cook, stirring occasionally, over medium heat until the vegetables soften and begin to brown, about 15 minutes. Add the garlic and half of the herbs and cook for 3 to 5 minutes more. Arrange the chicken, skin-side up, over the vegetables.

3. Add enough stock to come up to but not over the chicken and bring it to a simmer on top of the stove. Transfer the skillet to the oven and gently simmer, uncovered, for 1½ hours, adding more stock if the pan begins to look dry.

4. Add the artichokes, the remaining herbs, and the butter. Cook for another 15 minutes, basting the chicken frequently. When the chicken is done it will be very tender and well browned, and the braising liquid will have thickened slightly. Serve the chicken with the braising liquid and vegetables and garnish with additional fresh herbs.

artichoke and tomato gratin

SERVES 6 TO 8

4 tomatoes, halved

3 cups Onion Confit (page 235)

8 braised artichokes (page 129), thinly sliced

⅓ cup extra-virgin olive oil

Kosher salt and freshly ground black pepper

¼ cup Niçoise olives, pitted and finely chopped

4 anchovy fillets, finely chopped

¼ cup finely chopped fresh flat-leaf parsley

1 tablespoon fresh thyme leaves

1 Heat the oven to 375°F. Slice the tomato halves as thin as possible (they should be about the same thickness as the artichoke slices).

2. Spoon the Onion Confit into a medium baking dish in an even layer. Arrange the artichokes and tomatoes over the onions in a tightly overlapping pattern. Drizzle the gratin with 1 tablespoon of the olive oil, add salt and pepper, cover with aluminum foil, and bake for 30 minutes.

3. Reduce the oven temperature to 350°F., uncover the gratin, and continue cooking it until the tomatoes appear slightly dried, 20 to 30 minutes.

4. Just before serving, mix together ¼ cup of the olive oil, the olives, anchovies, parsley, and thyme leaves. Spoon this mixture evenly over the gratin and return it to the oven until it is heated through, about 10 minutes. Serve warm or at room temperature.

In this dish the braised artichokes are layered with onion confit, tomatoes, anchovies, and olives to make a side dish with complex but balanced flavors. The onions provide sweetness, the tomatoes lend their acidity, and the olives and anchovies bring saltiness to the dish.

trilogies

I'M A MUSIC LOVER. AS A LITTLE KID, I USED TO WALK THE STREETS of Elizabeth with a transistor radio, singing along to AM hits by groups like Edison Lighthouse and Mungo Jerry. I heard the Turtles' "Happy Together" for the first time in my father's barbershop, and I love it to this day. But no one beat the Beatles.

I was eight in 1970 when my father took us to see *Let It Be,* where we filled out ballots on whether or not the Fab Four should break up. Sad to say, my vote didn't count for much. As I worked on this book, I cooked along to the Beatles' *Anthology* album, marveling again at what Lennon and McCartney could do with the same twelve musical notes available to everyone else. I especially love the way the *Anthology* album takes a Beatles standard like "Strawberry Fields" and, starting with the earliest acoustic riff, builds to the finished song over the course of several tracks. Each version is slightly more developed than the last, but the essential melody stays the same. I saw this as an analogy to cooking. A full-blown dish rarely leaps into my mind; rather, it develops as a series of steps that build on each other, starting with a very basic through-line of ingredients.

Sometimes a limitless supply of alternatives can overwhelm rather than encourage.

This section is called "Trilogies" because I have deliberately limited myself to recipes with only three major ingredients, all seasonally in context with one another. Cooked simply, these three ingredients make an easy dish. Then I take the same three ingredients but work with them differently, to come up with different dishes. I hit upon this idea when I started teaching cooking classes, where I find the "limit" of three major ingredients actually frees people to come up with ideas. Sometimes a limitless supply of alternatives can overwhelm rather than encourage.

From intuition and experience I've found that certain foods simply work together, though again this is mostly Mother Nature's doing. I've played Lennon and chosen the basic melodies for you, each of which corresponds to a season. I hope you follow my lead and do the same, in your grocery or greenmarket. Find three ingredients that appear together seasonally and use them as the basis for your own trilogy.

asparagus, ramps, and morels

i CAN'T THINK OF A SINGLE VEGETABLE THAT HERALDS SPRING more than asparagus. It appears just as the last chill is subsiding and delivers promises of the riches to come. Lately, I've been noticing greenhouse (or imported) asparagus available all year, but the fresh stalks of spring are by far the best and can be had almost anywhere. The two other ingredients that make up this trilogy can be a little harder to find, which might be why they still aren't widely used by home cooks.

Morels are one of the great gifts of the mushroom family. They are elegant and earthy, with a distinctive nutty taste and a dark, honeycombed surface that acts as a sponge to soak up flavorful liquids. Of late they've become available at gourmet markets and specialty stores, as well as by mail order (see Resources, page 266). If you can't find them, you can substitute other varieties of wild mushrooms. However, most other mushrooms tend to cook more quickly than morels, so be alert.

Juxtaposed in interesting ways, these ingredients prove that the whole can be greater than the sum of its parts.

Leeks, for some reason, are treated like an exotic vegetable by home cooks in this country, despite the fact that they are widely available and deliver a milder, sweeter flavor than onions. Ramps are wild leeks, harvested only in the spring, and I prefer them for the reason I prefer wild varieties of almost everything: They taste like the cultivated variety, *only more so*. If you can't find ramps, you can substitute scallions or thin strips of leeks for the recipes in this section.

You'll notice that I like to experiment with texture in these recipes; asparagus become asparagus soup, morels make a decadent custard. Juxtaposed in interesting ways, these ingredients prove that the whole can be greater than the sum of its parts.

a note about cleaning

To clean thin asparagus, simply trim the dry bottoms and peel off any small leaves. For thicker stalks, hold one stalk on each end and bend, noting where it breaks naturally, then trim the rest in approximately the same place. Peel the woody stems, the way you'd peel a carrot.

Before washing morels, taste one first, and only wash if it tastes gritty, since washing saps them of some of their flavor. If they need it, drop the morels into a bowl of water and lift out with your hands, then blot dry on paper towels.

Cleaning a ramp is similar to cleaning a scallion. Start by peeling off the translucent outer layer. Trim the root and then cut down the leaves leaving about ¼ inch of green. Wash the ramps under cool, running water.

ragout of asparagus, ramps, and morels

SERVES 4

This recipe is great on its own or can be embellished with the addition of chopped, raw tomato or blanched peas.

¾ cup (1½ sticks) unsalted butter, chilled and cut into pieces
½ pound morels, cleaned, trimmed (page 148), halved or quartered if large
Kosher salt and freshly ground black pepper
¼ pound ramps, cleaned and trimmed (page 148)
1 pound asparagus, trimmed and cut into 2- to 3-inch pieces
1 tablespoon chopped fresh chervil (or fresh tarragon)
1 tablespoon chopped fresh chives

1. Bring about ½ inch of water (¼ to ½ cup) to a boil in a small saucepan over high heat. Reduce the heat to medium-low and whisk in the butter one piece at a time. (For more about beurre fondue, see page 77).

In this recipe we braise the vegetables in beurre fondue. This is the starting point for the recipes that follow in this section.

2. Transfer the beurre fondue to a medium saucepan and bring to a gentle simmer over medium heat. Add the morels a few at a time, then reduce the heat to low. Add salt and pepper and cook, stirring occasionally, until the morels begin to soften, 5 to 10 minutes. Add the ramps and continue to simmer gently until the morels are soft and the ramps tender, about 5 minutes more.

3. Meanwhile, cook the asparagus in a pot of boiling salted water until tender, 3 to 5 minutes. Drain the asparagus, then add them to the ragout. Add the chervil and chives and serve garnished with additional herbs if desired.

baked free-form "ravioli" with asparagus, ramps, and morels

SERVES 4 TO 8

This dish makes oversize, pillowy ravioli filled with cheese and finished with the ragout of asparagus, ramps, and morel. Don't try to make the ravioli into neat squares. They are meant to be loosely formed—just an easy fold of the pasta, and that's it. The recipe serves four as a main course or eight as an appetizer.

½ recipe (6 ounces) Basic Pasta Dough
   (page 165)
Kosher salt
1 pound ricotta cheese
1 cup freshly grated Parmigiano-
   Reggiano
2 tablespoons extra-virgin olive oil
Freshly ground black pepper

1 tablespoon chopped fresh chervil (or
   fresh basil)
1 recipe Ragout of Asparagus, Ramps,
   and Morels (page 149)
¼ cup mixed fresh herbs (such as
   chervil, chives, basil, flat-leaf parsley,
   and tarragon)

1. Use a pasta machine to roll out the dough. Work from the largest setting to the smallest, rolling the dough through each setting twice, and stopping short of the final setting. Lay out the rolled sheet of dough on a clean work surface. Cut the dough into 8 large squares. Place the pasta squares on a cookie sheet or cutting board dusted with cornmeal. Allow them to dry for about 5 minutes, then turn them and dry 5 minutes more. Bring a large pot of salted water to boil over high heat.

In this dish the braised spring vegetables are used as a sauce for the ravioli.

2. Heat the oven to 350°F. Mix the ricotta, ¾ cup of the Parmigiano-Reggiano, and the olive oil together in a medium saucepan. Add salt and pepper and warm the cheese mixture, stirring occasionally, over low heat.

3. Add the pasta squares to the boiling water one by one. Cook the squares just until they float to the surface, then drain, rinse under cold water, and pat dry. Set the pasta aside in a single layer on a cookie sheet lined with plastic wrap.

4. Mix the chervil into the cheese mixture. Place a heaping spoonful of the mixture in the center of a pasta square, then fold the pasta around the cheese, creating a little bundle. (There is no "correct" way to do this, just make sure that you don't use too much filling.) Gently place the ravioli, folded-side down, in an oiled baking dish. Repeat filling, folding, and transferring until you have filled all the squares.

5. Sprinkle the tops of the ravioli with the remaining ¼ cup of Parmigiano-Reggiano, and bake until the pasta is golden and slightly puffed, about 20 minutes.

6. Gently reheat the vegetable ragout over low heat. Place the ragout in shallow bowls, top with ravioli, and serve garnished with mixed fresh herbs.

sole with morels, ramps, and asparagus

SERVES 4

If you find the sauce in this recipe becoming too thick and small oil droplets forming toward the rim of the pan, add a few tablespoons of water.

¾ pound asparagus, trimmed and cut into 2- to 3-inch pieces
Kosher salt
1 cup (2 sticks) butter, chilled and cut into pieces
½ pound morels, cleaned and trimmed (page 148)
Freshly ground black pepper

¼ pound ramps, cleaned and trimmed (page 148)
1½ pounds fillet of sole, cut into 8 equal pieces
1 tablespoon chopped fresh chervil (or fresh tarragon)
1 tablespoon chopped fresh chives

1. Cook the asparagus in a pot of boiling salted water over high heat until tender but still bright green, 3 to 5 minutes. Remove the asparagus with a slotted spoon, plunge it into a bowl of cold water, drain, and set aside.

Here the ragout of asparagus, ramps, and morels becomes the braising medium for fish.

2. Bring about ½ inch of water (¼ to ½ cup) to a boil in a small saucepan over high heat. Reduce the heat to medium-low. Whisk the butter into the water one piece at a time. (For more about beurre fondue, see page 77.)

3. Transfer the beurre fondue to a large saucepan, raise the heat to medium, then add the morels a few at a time. Reduce the heat to low, add salt and pepper, and cook, stirring occasionally, until the morels begin to soften, 5 to 10 minutes. Add the ramps and gently simmer until the morels are soft and the ramps tender, about 5 minutes more.

4. Add the asparagus to the pan. Salt and pepper the fish and place it in the skillet, nestled among the vegetables. Cook at barely a simmer, basting the fish with the butter sauce, just until the fish flakes easily, about 5 minutes. Divide the ragout and fish among 4 shallow bowls, garnish with chervil and chives, and serve.

asparagus soup with morel custard

SERVES 8

FOR THE CUSTARD

2 tablespoons peanut oil

¼ pound morels, cleaned, trimmed (page 148), and coarsely chopped

1 or 2 ramps, white parts only, cleaned (page 148) and minced

Kosher salt and freshly ground black pepper

1 cup heavy cream

1 egg yolk

1 egg

FOR THE SOUP

2½ pounds asparagus

2 tablespoons peanut oil

2¼ cups White Chicken Stock (page 69)

2 shallots, peeled and minced

1 small leek, white part only, finely chopped

Kosher salt and freshly ground black pepper

¼ pound ramps, white parts only, cleaned, trimmed (page 148), and chopped

¼ cup heavy cream

3 tablespoons mixed fresh herbs (such as chervil, chives, tarragon, and basil)

1. Making the custard. Heat the oven to 325°F. and butter eight 2-ounce ramekins. Heat the oil in a medium skillet over medium-high heat until it slides easily across the pan. Add the morels, minced ramps, salt, and pepper, and cook until the morels begin to soften and release their juices, 3 to 5 minutes. Add the cream, bring it to a simmer, then reduce the heat to low and steep for about 10 minutes.

This dish plays with the texture of the vegetables while intensifying the flavors. The asparagus is puréed into soup, and the morels become a lush custard.

2. Strain the cream into a medium bowl; reserve the morels and ramps. Allow the cream to cool for 5 to 10 minutes. Beat the egg yolk and egg together, then add to the cream. Mix the custard well, then add a pinch of salt and the reserved morels and ramps.

3. Divide the custard among the ramekins. Place the ramekins in a large baking dish. Put the baking dish on the middle rack of the oven and add enough boiling water to come about half of the way up the ramekins. Cover the baking dish with aluminum foil and cook until the custard is set, 20 to 25 minutes.

4. **Making the soup.** While the custard bakes, cut the asparagus spears in half. Chop the tips and reserve, then chop the stems. Heat 1 tablespoon of the oil in a medium saucepan over medium heat until it moves easily across the pan. Add the stems and cook, stirring occasionally, until they start to soften, 5 to 10 minutes. Add the stock and bring it to a boil. Reduce the heat and gently simmer until the stock tastes like asparagus, about 15 minutes. Strain the infused stock and discard the cooked stems.

5. Heat the remaining tablespoonful of the oil in the saucepan over medium heat. Add the shallots, leek, salt, and pepper, and cook (without browning), stirring frequently, for 1 to 2 minutes. Add the asparagus tips and the ramps to the saucepan. Cook, stirring occasionally, until the asparagus tips begin to soften, about 10 minutes. Add the infused stock and simmer until the asparagus is soft but still bright green, about 5 minutes more. Add the cream.

6. Purée the soup, then press it through a fine strainer. Return the strained soup to the blender and blend until frothy (a handheld blender will also work).

7. **Assembling the dish.** Remove the custards from the oven and the ramekins from the baking dish. Set them aside just until they are cool enough to handle. Carefully run a knife around the outer rim of each ramekin. Unmold the custards into 8 shallow bowls. Ladle soup into the bowls and serve immediately, garnished with fresh herbs.

pan-roasted poussin with morels, ramps, and asparagus

SERVES 4

Poussin is a baby chicken, generally under a pound in weight. If poussin is not available, use a chicken cut into pieces.

2 tablespoons peanut oil
Kosher salt and freshly ground pepper
3 or 4 poussins (depending on size), quartered
½ pound morels, cleaned and trimmed (page 148)
½ pound ramps, cleaned and trimmed (page 148)

1 pound asparagus, trimmed and cut into 4-inch lengths
2 tablespoons unsalted butter
3 sprigs of fresh thyme
¼ pound sugar snap peas, trimmed and thinly sliced on the bias
¼ cup Brown Chicken Stock (page 70)

1. Heat the oil in a very large skillet over medium heat until it slides easily across the pan. Salt and pepper the poussins. Working in batches, brown the poussins, about 5 minutes per side, and set aside.

In this recipe we roast the morels, ramps, and asparagus along with the poussin to create an entirely new dish.

2. Add the morels to the skillet, then the ramps and asparagus. Add salt and pepper and cook, stirring frequently, until the morels begin to soften, 3 to 5 minutes.

3. Return the poussin legs to the skillet and add the butter and thyme. Cook for about 5 minutes, turning the poussins and vegetables in the melting butter (the asparagus should be bright green but not yet tender). Add the sugar snap peas and the poussin breasts and cook for 3 to 5 minutes more.

4. Add the stock, a tablespoon at a time, allowing each tablespoon to reduce to a glaze before adding the next. Continue cooking, turning the poussins and vegetables in the sauce, until all the stock has been added and the juices from the poussins run clear when pierced with a knife.

morel, ramp, and potato gratin

SERVES 4 TO 6

5 Idaho or other russet potatoes (about
    4 pounds), peeled and thinly sliced
3 cups heavy cream
Kosher salt and freshly ground black
    pepper

1 tablespoon peanut oil
½ pound ramps (about 2 bunches),
    trimmed and white parts only sliced
12 to 15 small morels, trimmed, washed
    (page 148), and halved or quartered

1. Heat the oven to 300°F. Place the potatoes in a medium saucepan and cover with the cream. Add salt and pepper and simmer over medium heat until the potatoes are just tender, about 15 minutes. Drain the potatoes, reserving the cream. Return the cream to the saucepan and simmer until the cream has reduced by half.

In this recipe the morels and potatoes are cooked first in cream and then baked with the ramps to form a gratin.

2. Heat the oil in a large skillet over medium heat until it slides easily across the pan. Add the ramps, salt, and pepper. Cook, stirring frequently, until the ramps are fragrant, about 1 minute, then add the morels. Cook, stirring occasionally, until the morels soften, about 5 minutes.

3. Add the morel mixture to the cream. Spoon half the potatoes into a medium baking dish; cover with half the cream and morel mixture. Repeat, spooning in the remaining potatoes, then covering with the remaining morel mixture. Bake the gratin until it is well browned, about 35 minutes, then serve.

There is no asparagus in this recipe, but it's so good I couldn't resist adding it.

lobster, peas, and pasta

PASTA WITH PEAS IS MY SON DANTE'S FAVORITE DISH (NO recipe needed, it's just what it sounds like, plus a little butter and salt). Instinctively he's grasped one of the best combinations I can think of, made even better with the addition of lobster. He likes his pasta with peas even when fresh peas aren't in season, so I keep a bag of frozen peas on hand in my home freezer. They work almost as well as fresh peas in these recipes.

Lobsters, on the other hand, have to be as fresh as possible. The best way to guarantee this is to buy them alive and kicking. I prefer to break up the lobsters before cooking them, since the claws and tails cook at a different rate. This also leaves the raw coral available for lobster butter and the unboiled shells for stock, which I reduce into lobster sauce.

The idea of homemade pasta seems to intimidate people; that is, until they've made it once. You can, of course, use dried pasta or packaged fresh pasta, which is widely available now instead. For ravioli, though, I think homemade is best, and it is less dry to work with than the packaged pasta sheets available commercially. If using packaged pasta sheets, refer to the directions on the package for cooking times.

Lobster, pasta, and peas could be prepared simply by boiling the ingredients separately, removing the lobster meat from the shell and chopping it, then tossing everything together with some extra-virgin olive oil and fresh herbs. The next step, in which we use some lobster stock to make a sauce for fettuccine, reinforces the lobster flavor and makes a more complete, satisfying dish without much additional effort.

basic boiled lobster

Although I'm partial to pan roasting lobster (page 49), this is the basic method by which to cook and extract lobster meat for use in other recipes. If pulling apart live lobsters doesn't appeal to you, plunge them into boiling water for about 1 minute, cool under cold running water, and then continue.

4 (1¼-pound) live lobsters   Kosher salt

Separate the tails and claws from the lobster bodies. Reserve the bodies for stock (page 71). Wrap the tails in a double layer of plastic wrap. Bring a large pot of salted water to a boil over high heat. Add the lobster tails, weighting (a heavy ceramic plate will work) and covering them. Cook the tails for 7 minutes, then remove them from the pot and rinse under cold water. Add the claws to the pot, weight, cover, and cook for 10 minutes. Drain the claws and rinse under cold water. Crack and serve the lobster or wrap the claws and tails in fresh plastic and refrigerate until ready to use (it is best to cook the lobster the same day you plan to eat it).

Wrapping the lobsters' tails in plastic allows them to cook in their own juices and retain optimal flavor.

fettuccine with lobster and peas

SERVES 4 TO 6

1 recipe Basic Pasta Dough (page 165)
Kosher salt
2 cups peas (about 2 pounds unshelled peas)
4 (1¼-pound) lobsters, boiled and shelled (page 163)
1½ cups Lobster Stock (page 71)

½ teaspoon tomato paste
1 cup heavy cream
Freshly ground black pepper
½ cup (1 stick) unsalted butter
2 tablespoons chopped fresh dill
2 tablespoons chopped fresh chives

1. Divide the pasta into 6 equal parts. Roll out the first piece in a pasta machine, working from the largest setting to the smallest and rolling the dough through each setting twice. Lay the pasta sheet on a clean work surface and dry for about 5 minutes; turn and dry for 5 minutes more. Cut the dough using the fettuccine attachment to the pasta machine (this can also be done with a sharp knife), then set the fettuccine aside in coils on a cookie sheet. Repeat, rolling, drying, and cutting the remaining dough.

2. Bring a pot of salted water to a boil over high heat. Cook the peas in the water until tender, 3 to 5 minutes. Drain, then rinse the peas under cold water. Set aside. Cut the lobster into large pieces.

3. Bring the stock to a simmer in a medium saucepan over medium heat. Add the tomato paste and reduce by about two-thirds. Whisk in the cream, then simmer the mixture until the sauce has reduced enough to coat the back of a spoon, about 10 minutes. Add salt and pepper and keep the sauce warm over very low heat, stirring occasionally.

4. Meanwhile, bring about ½ inch (¼ to ½ cup) of water to a boil in a medium saucepan. Reduce the heat to medium-low. Whisk the butter into the simmering water a piece at a time (for more information on beurre fondue, see page 77). Add the lobster, season with salt and pepper, and warm the lobster over very low heat.

5. Bring a large pot of salted water to a boil over high heat. Add the pasta and cook until just tender, about 3 minutes. Drain the pasta, then combine it with the lobster, peas, lobster sauce, dill, and chives. Mix gently, taste for salt and pepper, and serve.

basic pasta dough

MAKES 12 OUNCES

2 eggs, lightly beaten
1 tablespoon extra-virgin olive oil

2 cups all-purpose flour
Pinch of salt

Combine the eggs, olive oil, and 1 tablespoon water in a small bowl and mix well. Combine the flour and salt in a large bowl. Make a well in the center of the flour mixture and pour in the egg mixture. Gradually work the flour mixture into the egg mixture until the dough holds together, adding up to 1 more tablespoon water if necessary. Transfer the dough to a clean work surface and knead until it is smooth and elastic. Wrap the dough in plastic, and refrigerate for at least 1 hour but not longer than 2 days. Roll out according to the specific recipe instructions.

chilled pea soup with lobster, pasta, and pea salad

SERVES 6

FOR THE SOUP

Kosher salt

5½ cups shelled peas (5 to 6 pounds unshelled)

1 tablespoon peanut oil

2 shallots, peeled and minced

1 small leek, white part only, trimmed and minced

3 cups heavy cream

Freshly ground black pepper

FOR THE SALAD

2 (1¼-pound) lobsters, boiled and shelled (page 163)

¼ pound orzo

Kosher salt

2 tablespoons extra-virgin olive oil

1 tablespoon chopped fresh chives

1 tablespoon chopped fresh chervil plus additional sprigs for garnish (substitute fresh flat-leaf parsley if chervil is unavailable)

1 loosely packed cup of pea shoots (optional)

Freshly ground black pepper

1. Bring a large pot of salted water to a boil over high heat. Add the peas and cook until tender, 3 to 5 minutes. Rinse under cold water and set aside.

> This dish highlights the peas, by turning them into soup. The lobster and pasta take a secondary role as a refreshing salad.

2. Making the soup. Heat the oil in a medium saucepan over medium heat until it slides easily across the pan. Add the shallots and leek and cook, stirring occasionally, until they begin to soften, about 5 minutes. Add 4½ cups of the peas and cook until they are soft but still bright green, 2 to 3 minutes. Add the cream, salt, and pepper and simmer, stirring occasionally, for about 5 minutes. Cool slightly.

3. Transfer the soup in batches to a blender and purée. Press the soup through a fine strainer, then blend again. Chill the soup until ready to serve.

4. Making the salad. Chop the lobster meat. Cook the orzo in boiling salted water until tender. Drain the orzo and combine it with 1 tablespoon of the olive oil, the lobster, and the remaining cup of peas in a medium bowl. Mix well. Add the chives, chervil, and pea shoots. Add salt, pepper, and the remaining olive oil and mix gently.

5. Assembling the dish. Arrange salad in the center of 6 soup bowls. Spoon the soup around the salad and garnish with sprigs of chervil.

spiced roasted lobster with pea ravioli

SERVES 4 TO 6

FOR THE RAVIOLI
Kosher salt
2½ cups peas (2 to 3 pounds unshelled
    peas)
1 tablespoon peanut oil
1 shallot, peeled and minced
½ cup heavy cream
Freshly ground black pepper
1 recipe Basic Pasta Dough (page 165)
Cornmeal

FOR THE SAUCE
1½ cups Lobster Stock (page 71)
1 teaspoon Lobster Spice (page 173)
Zest of ½ orange, cut into thin strips
Small piece of fresh ginger, peeled and
    smashed
4 green cardamom pods
3 tablespoons crème fraîche

2 tablespoons Lobster Butter (page 173)
Kosher salt
2 teaspoons red peppercorns

FOR THE ROASTED LOBSTER
4 (1¼-pound) live lobsters, tails and
    claws removed, bodies reserved
    for stock
Kosher salt
1 tablespoon extra-virgin olive oil
½ teaspoon Lobster Spice (page 173)
5 tablespoons unsalted butter
2 bay leaves
1 tablespoon chopped fresh chervil or
    tarragon
1 tablespoon chopped fresh chives
½ cup loosely packed pea shoots
    (optional)

1. Making the ravioli. Bring a large pot of salted water to a boil over high heat. Cook the peas in the water until tender, 3 to 5 minutes. Drain them, then rinse under cold water. Set the peas aside.

2. Heat the oil in a medium saucepan over medium heat until it slides easily across the pan. Add the shallots and cook, stirring occasionally, until they begin to soften, about 5 minutes. Add 1½ cups of the peas and cook until they are soft but still bright green, 2 to 3 minutes. (Reserve the remaining peas for finishing the dish.) Add the cream, salt, and pepper and simmer, stirring occasionally, for about 5 minutes. Cool slightly. Transfer to a blender and purée. Press the purée through a strainer and set aside.

3. Divide the pasta dough in half. Roll out the first half in a pasta machine. Work from the largest setting to the smallest, rolling the dough through each setting twice. Stop short of the final setting. Lay out the rolled sheet of dough on a clean work surface. Using half the pea purée, place spoonfuls in two rows of three over half the pasta sheet (there should be about 2 inches between each spoonful). Brush the other half of the sheet lightly with water, then fold it over the first. Run your fingers around each pocket of filling, pressing to seal, then cut the ravioli into squares or rounds. Transfer the ravioli to a baking sheet dusted with cornmeal. Repeat with remaining dough and filling. Set the filled ravioli aside to dry for about 15 minutes, then turn them over and dry for 15 minutes more.

4. Preparing the sauce. Combine the stock, Lobster Spice, orange zest, ginger, and cardamom pods in a medium saucepan. Bring the mixture to a simmer and reduce by about two-thirds. Remove the spiced stock from the heat and steep for about 10 minutes. Strain the stock through a fine sieve. Wipe out the pan, return the stock, and bring it to a gentle simmer over medium heat. Whisk in the crème fraîche, simmer the sauce a minute or two, then reduce the heat to low. Whisk the Lobster Butter into the sauce, a piece at a time, then add salt. Keep the sauce warm over very low heat, stirring occasionally.

> Here we partially cook the lobster by boiling it first, then finish later by roasting it, which intensifies the flavor. This combination method is my favorite technique for cooking lobster.

5. Parboiling the lobster. Wrap the lobster tails in a double layer of plastic wrap. Bring a large pot of salted water to a boil over high heat. Parboil the tails in the water, weighted (a heavy ceramic plate will work) and covered, for 4 minutes, then rinse them under cold water and unwrap. Parboil the claws for 7 minutes, then rinse under cold water. Crack the claws and tails, remove the meat (discarding the tail vein), and set aside.

6. Finishing the dish. Refill the pot with salted water and bring it to a boil over high heat. Cook the ravioli in the water until tender, about 3 minutes, then drain the ravioli, reserving about ¼ cup of the cooking water.

7. Heat the olive oil in a large skillet over medium-high heat until it shimmers. Sprinkle the lobster with salt and Lobster Spice and add it to the skillet. Cook the lobster for 30 seconds, then add 2 tablespoons of the butter. Turn the lobster, cook 30 seconds longer, then reduce the heat to low. Add 2 more tablespoons of

the butter and the bay leaves and cook, turning the lobster in the butter until the meat is just firm, about 3 minutes total.

8. Arrange the lobster in large serving bowls. Discard the bay leaves and wipe out the skillet. Melt the remaining tablespoon of butter with a little of the pasta cooking water over medium-low heat. Add the ravioli, reserved peas, and half the chopped chervil and chives. Warm the ravioli and peas. Mix the warm lobster sauce with a handheld mixer or froth it in the blender. Add the red peppercorns to the sauce and spoon it around the lobster. Divide the ravioli and peas among the bowls and garnish with the reserved herbs and pea shoots if desired.

lobster risotto with peas

Kosher salt
1 cup peas, shelled
6 to 8 cups Lobster Stock (page 71)
2 tablespoons olive oil
1 onion, peeled and diced
1½ cups Arborio or other short-grain
   rice

Freshly ground black pepper
2 (1¼-pound) lobsters, boiled (page
   163), and chopped
1 tablespoon unsalted butter

1. Bring a large pot of salted water to a boil over high heat. Add the peas and cook until tender, 3 to 5 minutes. Rinse under cold water and set aside.

2. Bring the lobster stock to a simmer in a medium saucepan over medium-high heat. Reduce the heat to low and keep warm.

3. Heat the oil in a medium saucepan over medium heat until it moves easily across the pan. Add the onion and cook, stirring occasionally, until soft, about 15 minutes. Add the rice, salt, and pepper and cook, stirring, until the rice is heated through and slightly translucent, about 1 minute.

4. Add enough stock to almost cover the rice, about 2 cups. Simmer, stirring frequently, until the rice is almost dry, 5 to 10 minutes. Stir in another cup of stock and cook, stirring, until the rice is once again dry. Continue to gradually add the stock, cooking and stirring until the rice is tender and creamy, about 25 minutes. Add the peas, lobster, and butter, while stirring. Taste for salt and pepper, and serve.

lobster spice

MAKES ABOUT 2 TEASPOONS

This fragrant spice mixture can be used on just about any roasted fish, but it seems to lend itself particularly to lobster. (See Spiced Roasted Lobster with Pea Ravioli, page 168.)

½ teaspoon mustard seed
½ teaspoon coriander seed
½ teaspoon fennel seed

1 bay leaf, crumbled
Pinch of cayenne pepper

Toast the mustard, coriander, and fennel seeds over medium-low heat in a small skillet until fragrant. Transfer the toasted spices to a grinder or mortar. Add the bay leaf and cayenne and grind. Store the spice mix in an airtight container until ready to use.

lobster butter

MAKES ½ CUP

Roe from 1 or 2 lobsters
¼ pound (1 stick) unsalted butter,
    softened

Kosher salt

Place the roe, butter, and a pinch of salt in a food processor or blender and purée until the mixture is smooth. Lay a square of plastic wrap, about 5 × 5 inches, on a clean surface. Spoon the lobster butter onto the plastic. Mold the butter into a cylinder as you wrap it tightly. Chill before using. Lobster butter can be kept in the refrigerator for 1 to 2 days or for up to a month in the freezer.

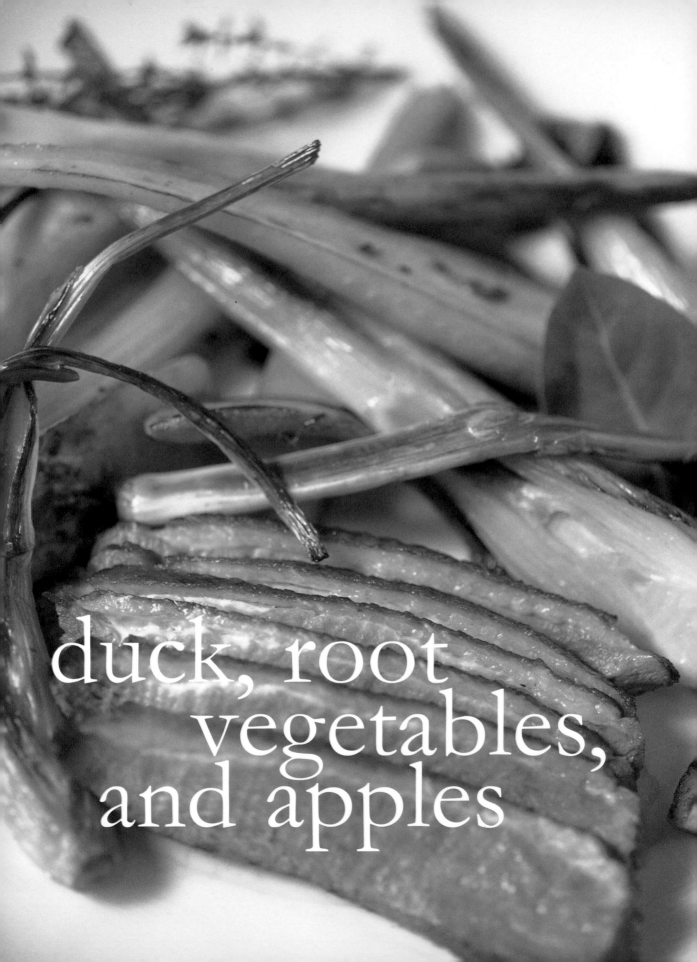

duck, root
vegetables,
and apples

HOW COULD THESE THREE THINGS NOT GO TOGETHER? EACH for me pulls up a visceral image of autumn, of weather turning crisp and days getting shorter and, not coincidentally, food getting heartier for the coming winter months. The root vegetables and apples are a perfect example of my favorite maxim, "What grows together goes together."

Because the breast and legs of the duck cook so differently, this trilogy really lets you experiment with texture in your recipes. I love the idea of taking duck beyond its traditional preparation and braising it, confiting it in its own fat, or curing it with spices to make a "ham." The apple in these recipes picks up on the starchy sweetness of root vegetables and makes them even more of a comfort food.

a note about the ingredients

Any type of duck will work in these recipes, but they are slightly different from one another. If your supermarket carries duck, it is likely to be Pekin, your basic Long Island duck (not to be confused with Peking duck, which is a Chinese preparation). Pekin ducks tend to have a high amount of fat—so much that the leg practically confits itself when it roasts (this is a good thing). If you are looking to roast a whole duck and want a crispy skin, Pekin duck is the one to choose.

I prefer Muscovy ducks, as they are more flavorful than Pekin, with less fat and a darker, richer meat. The breasts also tend to be larger—especially in the males—so ask for a male Muscovy duck at the butcher or meat counter. Magret refers to the breast of Moullard ducks, which have been fattened for foie gras. (Moullards are a cross between a Mallard and a Muscovy.) Mallard ducks are wild and delicious, but difficult to find, unless you're friendly with a hunter. You can buy just the breast, or just the breast and the legs, depending on what the recipe calls for, or buy the whole bird and roast it as you would a chicken. When buying a duck breast, make sure the meat is a nice, rosy pink. If it appears at all brown, the meat is no longer fresh.

I like the flavor of Granny Smith apples, which is why I call for them in these recipes. The water content of various apples, which is important in baking, is less important here, so feel free to use whatever apples you have available. Root vegetables are best after the first frost; the cold helps to convert the starches into sugar. If you can't find the exact root vegetables a recipe calls for, substitute more of another instead. The proportions here are what matter, rather than the specific vegetable.

Apples at Union Square Greenmarket.

roasted duck, root vegetables, and apples

SERVES 4

2 parsnips, peeled

2 leeks, white part only, trimmed

2 medium carrots, peeled

2 tablespoons duck fat (page 183)

2 fennel bulbs, quartered lengthwise

4 turnips, peeled and quartered

12 pearl onions, peeled

Kosher salt and freshly ground black
pepper

2 Granny Smith apples, cored

4 (8-ounce) boneless duck breasts

Coarse sea salt (optional)

1. Heat the oven to 375°F. Cut the parsnips, leeks, and carrots into lengths (½ × 3 inches). Heat the duck fat in a large skillet over medium heat until it slides easily across the pan. Add the parsnips, leeks, carrots, fennel, turnips, and pearl onions and season with salt and pepper. Cook, turning frequently, until they begin to brown, about 5 minutes, then transfer to a baking dish large enough to hold them in a single layer.

2. Roast in the oven, turning occasionally, until they begin to soften, about 30 minutes. Quarter the apples and add them to the vegetables.

3. Meanwhile, place the duck breasts, skin-side up, on a cutting board. Make shallow crosshatch incisions just through the layer of fat (don't cut into the meat) with a sharp knife. Wipe out the skillet, and heat over medium. Salt and pepper the duck breasts and add them to the skillet, skin-side down. Cook the breasts until the skins are crisp and the fat largely rendered, about 5 minutes. Turn and cook for 1 minute more.

4. Place the duck breasts on top of the roasting vegetables, skin-side up. Continue to roast until the breasts are medium rare and the vegetables very tender, about 5 minutes more.

5. Transfer the duck breasts to a cutting board and allow them to rest for 5 to 10 minutes. Keep the vegetables warm in a low oven. Slice the duck breasts lengthwise into long pieces about ¼ inch thick. Serve the slices over the vegetables sprinkled with coarse salt if desired (See photograph on page 174).

braised duck with apples

SERVES 4

2 tablespoons peanut oil
Kosher salt and freshly ground black
  pepper
4 duck legs with thighs
4 duck wings, tip joint trimmed off
1 large onion, peeled and quartered
3 carrots, peeled and coarsely chopped
3 celery stalks, peeled and coarsely
  chopped
4 garlic cloves, peeled

2 sprigs of fresh thyme
2 sprigs of fresh tarragon
About 1 cup Brown Chicken Stock
  (page 70)
2 Granny Smith apples, cored and
  quartered
2 tablespoons unsalted butter
1 tablespoon chopped fresh thyme
1 tablespoon chopped fresh tarragon

1. Heat the oven to 350°F. Heat the oil in a large ovenproof skillet over medium-high heat until it shimmers. Salt and pepper the duck legs and wings on both sides, then, working in batches, brown the duck, about 5 minutes per side. Set aside.

Here the duck and apples are braised together, flavoring each other in the process.

2. Pour off all but enough fat to coat the skillet. Add the onion, carrots, celery, and a little salt. Cook over medium heat, stirring occasionally, until the vegetables soften and begin to brown, about 15 minutes. Add the garlic and the sprigs of thyme and tarragon. Cook until the vegetables are almost tender, 3 to 5 minutes more.

3. Arrange the duck, skin-side up, over the vegetables. Add enough stock to cover the vegetables but not the duck. Bring the stock to a simmer.

4. Add the apples and transfer the skillet to the oven. Gently simmer—just an occasional bubble—basting occasionally, until the duck is very tender and well browned, about 2 hours.

5. Remove the duck from the pan and cover loosely with aluminum foil. Strain the braising liquid, pressing the vegetables and apples with a wooden spoon. Discard the vegetables and apples and return the liquid to the skillet. Bring it to a simmer and skim off the fat.

6. Whisk the butter and chopped thyme and tarragon into the braising liquid. Return the duck to the skillet, heat through, then serve.

root vegetable and apple ragout with duck crepes

SERVES 4

Note that this recipe calls for adding the stock a small amount at a time. This keeps the pan from cooling down, so that the flavors in the vegetables and apples remain bright.

8 crepes (page 180)
½ small head of Savoy cabbage, cored
1 carrot, peeled
1 leek, white part only, trimmed and halved
1 fennel bulb, cored and halved
1 parsnip, peeled
1 garlic clove, peeled
1 sweet potato, peeled
1 Granny Smith apple, peeled and cored
2 turnips, peeled
1 onion, peeled

5 tablespoons peanut oil
Kosher salt and freshly ground black pepper
1½ cups White Chicken Stock (page 69) or water
2 tablespoons unsalted butter
2 tablespoons chopped mixed fresh herbs (such as thyme, savory, flat-leaf parsley, and rosemary)
2½ cups shredded Duck Confit (page 183)

1. Heat the oven to 200° F. Wrap the crepes in aluminum foil and warm them in the oven while you prepare the ragout.

In this recipe we use two different techniques to complete the dish: We braise the vegetables with the apples and confit the duck.

2. Separate the leaves of cabbage and tear them into small pieces. Thinly slice the carrot, leek, fennel, parsnip, and garlic. Quarter, then thinly slice the sweet potato, apple, turnips, and onion.

3. Heat 3 tablespoons of the oil in a large saucepan over medium-high heat until it shimmers. Add the vegetables, a handful at a time, first the onion and garlic, then carrot, fennel, sweet potato, turnips, parsnip, leek, apple, and cabbage. The pan should always be sizzling but never smoking—adjust the heat accordingly. Salt and pepper the vegetables and cook, stirring, until the vegetables have all been added and the cabbage is wilted.

4. Add the stock ¼ cup at a time, bringing each addition to a simmer before adding more. Stir gently but continuously so the ragout cooks evenly. Once all the stock has been added, stir in the butter, herbs, salt, and pepper. Cook until the butter melts and the vegetables are just tender. Keep the ragout warm over very low heat.

5. Meanwhile, warm the confit in a small skillet or saucepan over low heat.

6. Divide the confit among the crepes. Fold or roll the crepes around the filling. Heat the remaining 2 tablespoons of oil over medium heat in a medium skillet. Lightly brown the crepes, about 2 minutes. Divide the ragout among 4 plates or shallow bowls, top each portion with 2 crepes, and serve.

basic crepes

MAKES ABOUT EIGHT 8½-INCH CREPES

½ cup flour
½ cup milk
¼ cup lukewarm water
2 eggs, beaten

2 tablespoons unsalted butter, melted
   and cooled
½ teaspoon kosher salt
3 tablespoons peanut oil

1. Combine the flour, milk, water, eggs, butter, and salt in a blender and mix until smooth. Cover the batter and refrigerate it for at least 30 minutes.

2. Heat a crepe pan or small nonstick skillet over medium heat. Add just enough oil to barely coat the surface, about ½ tablespoon. Stir the batter and pour about 2 tablespoons into the skillet and cook until the top of the crepe is set and the bottom is golden. Turn the crepe over and cook for a few seconds longer, then transfer it to a plate. Repeat, adding oil as necessary, and stack the finished crepes separated by layers of parchment or wax paper. Cover the crepes with a clean dish towel to keep warm.

From left: Duck Ham (recipe, page 185), Duck Confit, Duck Rillettes (recipe, page 185).

duck confit

This dish always brings to mind a ski trip I took with my friend George Faisan to Vail. The duck confit he brought along, shredded, made a great filling for burritos, which we ate right on top of the mountain. Start this recipe a day ahead: The duck needs to cure for 24 hours before cooking.

3 tablespoons kosher salt
4 garlic cloves, smashed
1 shallot, peeled and sliced
6 sprigs of fresh thyme

4 duck legs with thighs
4 duck wings, tip joint trimmed off
Coarsely ground black pepper
About 4 cups duck fat

1. Sprinkle 1 tablespoon of the salt in the bottom of a dish large enough to hold the duck pieces in a single layer. Evenly scatter half the garlic, shallot, and thyme over the salt. Place the duck on top of the salt mixture, then sprinkle with the remaining salt, garlic, shallot, and thyme. Season with pepper, cover with plastic wrap, and refrigerate for 24 hours.

"Confit" is the French term for preserve. The confit recipe calls for a fair amount of duck fat, which you might be able to get from the whole ducks if you cut them up yourself, from a butcher, or by mail order from d'Artagnan, 1-800-DAR-TAGN.

2. Heat the oven to 225°F. Melt the duck fat in a saucepan over medium-low heat. Brush the salt and seasonings off the duck and arrange the pieces in a single snug layer in a high-sided baking dish. Pour the melted fat over the duck. (The duck pieces should be covered by fat. If they are not, switch pans or use more fat.) Transfer the confit to the oven and cook at a very gentle simmer—just an occasional bubble—until the duck is tender and can be easily pulled from the bone, 2 to 3 hours. Remove the dish from the oven and set aside to cool. Store the duck in the fat in the refrigerator, up to 1 month.

3. To use, brown the duck pieces, skin-side down, in a small amount of fat, turn over, and place in a 300°F. oven until heated through, about 15 minutes.

root vegetable soup with apples and duck ham

1 Granny Smith apple, cored
Juice of ½ lemon
2 tablespoons peanut oil
½ fennel bulb, cored and thinly sliced
1 medium carrot, peeled and thinly sliced
1 small onion, peeled and thinly sliced
1 small leek, white part only, trimmed and thinly sliced
1 butternut squash, peeled and thinly sliced

1 parsnip, peeled and sliced
1 garlic clove, peeled and sliced
Kosher salt and freshly ground black pepper
2 sprigs of fresh thyme
2 tablespoons unsalted butter
About 4 cups White Chicken Stock (page 69) or water, warmed
1 (8-ounce) Duck Ham (page 185), thinly sliced then cut into lengths

1. Cut half the apple into thin lengths about 2 inches long and ¹⁄₁₆ inch thick. Set the apple strips aside in a bowl of ice water mixed with the lemon juice. Thinly slice the remaining apple. Heat the oil in a large saucepan over medium heat until it slides easily across the pan. Add the sliced apple, fennel, carrot, onion, leek, squash, parsnip, and garlic. Add salt and pepper and cook, stirring occasionally, until the vegetables begin to soften, about 15 minutes.

Here the root vegetables and apples are puréed into a hearty soup, then garnished with duck ham (page 185).

2. Add the thyme and 1 tablespoon of the butter and continue cooking until the vegetables are tender, about 5 minutes more. Begin gradually adding 3 cups of the stock or water, about ½ cup at a time, bringing the soup to a simmer before each addition. Reduce the heat to medium-low and continue cooking until the vegetables are very soft, about 40 minutes total. Remove and discard the thyme.

3. Allow the soup to cool for 5 to 10 minutes, then purée in batches in a blender or food processor. Return the soup to the pan and thin with up to 1 cup of the remaining stock or water. Taste for salt and pepper, and gently reheat. Stir in the remaining butter and serve garnished with the reserved apple and duck ham.

duck ham

This recipe is essentially prosciutto, only with duck instead of pork.

2 (8-ounce) duck breasts

2 cups kosher salt

½ cup sugar

3 garlic cloves, peeled and chopped

2 tablespoons freshly ground black pepper

1 tablespoon fresh thyme leaves

3 bay leaves, crumbled

1. Place the duck breasts in the freezer for 15 to 20 minutes. Using a sharp knife, remove the skin and most of the fat, leaving only a thin protective layer.

2. Mix the salt, sugar, garlic, pepper, thyme, and bay leaves. Lay two pieces of plastic wrap on a clean work surface. Place a quarter of the salt mixture on each piece of plastic. Lay the duck breasts, skin-side down, on the salt, then cover with the remaining salt mixture. Wrap each breast tightly and refrigerate for 24 hours.

3. Unwrap the duck hams, discard the salt mixture, and blot dry with paper towels. Slice and serve or wrap in fresh plastic and refrigerate until ready to use.

duck rillettes

This recipe works for the terrine, which follows, but is delicious seasoned with plenty of pepper and served by itself with toasted country bread.

4 to 5 cups shredded Duck Confit (page 183)

¼ cup duck fat plus additional for sealing

Place the duck confit in a food processor and add 1 tablespoon of the duck fat. Pulse the machine just until the meat is chopped, adding enough of the remaining fat so the rillettes hold together.

duck, root vegetable, and apple terrine

MAKES 1 TERRINE (SERVES 12 TO 14 AS AN APPETIZER)

This recipe combines all the techniques in this chapter. It's time-consuming, but well worth the effort.

1 large carrot, peeled

1 sweet potato, peeled

1 parsnip, peeled

1 Granny Smith apple, peeled and cored

1 small celery root, peeled

2 tablespoons duck fat

Kosher salt and freshly ground black pepper

1 small head of Savoy cabbage, cored, leaves separated, and ribs removed

4 braised duck legs with braising liquid (page 178)

2 duck breasts, skin and fat removed

1 to 2 cups Brown Chicken Stock (page 70)

2 teaspoons powdered gelatin (1 ¼-ounce packet)

½ cup Duck Rillettes (page 185)

1. Preheat the oven to 375°F. Cut the carrot, sweet potato, parsnip, apple, and celery root into lengths about 2½ inches long and ¼ inch to ½ inch thick. Heat the duck fat in a large ovenproof skillet over medium heat until it slides easily across the pan. Add the vegetables to the skillet. Add salt and pepper and cook, turning the vegetables frequently, until they begin to brown, about 5 minutes.

2. Transfer the skillet to the oven and roast the vegetables, turning them occasionally, until they are tender, 30 to 40 minutes. Remove the vegetables from the oven and set aside to cool.

3. Cook the cabbage leaves in a large pot of boiling salted water until tender, 3 to 5 minutes. Drain the leaves, then rinse and thoroughly dry them.

4. Strain the braised duck, reserving the braising liquid. Bring the liquid to a simmer in a small saucepan. Skim off the fat, then set aside to cool. Shred the braised duck meat, discarding the skin and bones. Set the meat aside.

5. Season the duck breasts with salt and pepper. Cook them over high heat in a large skillet until rare, about 2 minutes per side. Set aside to cool.

6. Combine the braising liquid with enough stock to measure 2¼ cups. Pour the mixture into a small saucepan and sprinkle with gelatin, then dissolve according to the instructions on the gelatin packet.

7. Line a 5-cup terrine with plastic wrap. Arrange the cabbage leaves so they completely cover the bottom and sides of the mold and drape about 4 inches over the sides. Distribute about one-third of the braised duck over the bottom of the terrine, top with about half the roasted vegetables, and cover with all of the rillettes. Fit the two seared duck breasts into the terrine end to end. Top the breasts with another third of the braised duck and the remaining vegetables. End with a final layer of braised duck, then pour the gelatin mixture over the terrine. Fold the cabbage leaves over the top. Cover with plastic wrap, then weight the terrine and refrigerate at least 24 hours. Unmold, slice, and serve.

It is important to weight the terrine evenly while it sits in the refrigerator. I like to cut a few pieces of rigid cardboard wrapped in foil to fit snugly inside the terrine dish over the duck, which I then weight down with a box of kosher salt or a bottle of wine.

component
cooking

S PRING 1989. I WAS TWENTY-SEVEN YEARS OLD, WORKING LONG days and nights at Mondrian to establish my reputation. Word came from reservations that a famous French chef was coming in that evening to dine.

I planned an elaborate tasting menu, excited at the chance to show this seasoned pro what a young American chef could do with the wealth of fresh ingredients that were coming into the marketplace at the time. I watched in the kitchen as dish after dish returned from his table, all but scraped clean.

At the close of his meal, I approached the great chef with some nervousness, but also a sense of satisfaction. I knew I had done my best, and he had eaten well. "Wonderful, wonderful," he enthused, shaking my hand.

"But zere ees one zing, Tom," he rasped in his gravelly voice. "Everyzing you give to me, eet ees *green*. Green zees, green zat. How come so many green vegetables?"

I paused, not sure if this was a test of some kind. "Well . . ." I said, choosing my words carefully. "It's *spring*."

I saw him thinking this over. Great, I thought. I blew it. Two minutes later he offered me a job.

If it grows together, it goes together.

You may have noticed by now that to me, cooking is intensely seasonal. You don't have to start out with an advanced understanding of what ingredient goes with what, since the tough thinking has been done for you by Mother Nature. I like to sum up my philosophy like this: If it grows together, it goes together.

By now I've walked you through the techniques I feel are essential to let you approach any ingredient with confidence. I've tried to give you an understanding of a chef's creative paradigm—working from one simple ingredient outward to many—and, with the section on Trilogies, a chance to see how a chef plays with one natural combination to build many different dishes. Now I'd like to introduce a concept that I rely upon in my restaurants (and at home, for that matter) to create combinations. I call it component cooking.

how components make a menu

As I plan the menu in my restaurants, I view the elements in each dish as separate components, each bringing its own essential nature and nuance to the plate. By and large the protein in the dish—the meat, fish, or poultry—is a fixed component and varies little throughout the year. Vegetables, on the other hand, change wildly from season to season and vastly alter the landscape of the menu as they come and go. Sauces, chutneys, and relishes (most often vegetable-based) are yet another variable component that can be used to reinforce the flavors of a dish or to introduce an entirely new flavor altogether.

Where I am asked to use my skill as a chef is in layering or juxtaposing the components in a dish to maximum effect. I know the vegetable combinations that don't belong together, because they just don't feel right: Watermelon and parsnips. Bell pepper and quince. Here, again, the maxim applies: What grows together goes together. Right now, as I write this, beautiful fall figs, fennel, and endive have appeared in the marketplace. You don't have to be a chef to know they will roast together magically.

I don't see a dish of fennel, figs, and endive as a side dish, necessarily, but as a component in its own right. I can serve it with equal success by itself as a dish on Gramercy's vegetable tasting menu or alongside roasted meat or chicken, even roasted fish. In my opinion, just about any protein with strong, roasted flavors to stand up to the rich, caramelized flavors of the vegetables will work.

The following series of recipes, broken down by season, are intended to be used as components as you design your own meals. Some rely upon simple techniques. Others—such as some of the chutneys—are slightly more involved, but are worth the extra effort for the way they elevate an entire dish. If at times my use of a certain vegetable seems repetitive, it is; I prefer to use seasonal vegetables in a variety of ways, rather than search for exotic or out-of-season ingredients that aren't at their best.

Swiss Chard

★ A MEMBER OF THE BEET FAMILY, GOOD STEAMED OR STIRFRIED.

$1.³⁰ per ½ lb.

spring
vegetables

SPRINGTIME IN NEW YORK CITY IS MORE THAN JUST A CHANGE in weather, it's a change in attitude. You can almost hear the collective sigh of relief as curbside snow yields to puddles, and our intermittent trees bud. The feeling of anticipation is everywhere. At the same time, the greenmarkets start to come alive, with vegetables appearing that tickle the senses in subtle ways, unlike the full-blown scene-stealers of summer. Spring onions and ramps, garlic shoots and wild mushrooms. Or asparagus, which I buy in every form available: thin, thick, white, and wild. I especially like to try to use different techniques on these vegetables to bring out optimal flavor. Fresh asparagus, blanched or steamed, is delicious. But pan roasting asparagus intensifies the flavor without much more effort. See page 203 for that recipe.

pickled ramps

To lengthen the ramps' short season, I pickle them in this sweet-and-sour brine, which allows them to keep for months. They work well with roasted fish or meats, and the pickling liquid, reduced and added to crème fraîche, makes a delicious sauce for soft-shell crabs (page 48).

1 cup white wine vinegar
1 cup sugar
1 teaspoon mustard seed
1 teaspoon coriander seed
1 teaspoon fennel seed

1 teaspoon red peppercorns
1 bay leaf
2 pounds ramps, cleaned and trimmed
   (page 148)
Kosher salt

1. Combine the vinegar and sugar with 1 cup of water in a saucepan and bring to a boil. Add the mustard, coriander, and fennel seeds as well as the peppercorns and bay leaf. Keep warm over low heat.

2. Meanwhile, cook the ramps in a large pot of boiling salted water until almost tender, about 3 minutes. Drain, then rinse the ramps under cold water. Place them in a large bowl or jar. Pour the hot vinegar mixture over the ramps and set aside to cool. Cover and refrigerate for at least 3 days before serving.

Ramps are indigenous wild leeks that go way back in this country—there's even a reference in *Huckleberry Finn* to "eating ramp." They have long been popular in rural West Virginia, home of the Annual Ramp Festival. Despite this, chefs largely ignored them until about ten years ago; as wild ingredients became more popular, they found their way into the greenmarket, and from there onto restaurant tables.

pan-roasted ramps

Ramps have a pungent, garlicky flavor that mellows considerably when they are roasted.

1 tablespoon peanut oil	Kosher salt and freshly ground black
2 pounds ramps, cleaned and trimmed	pepper
(page 148)	1 tablespoon unsalted butter

Heat the oil in a large skillet over medium-high heat until it shimmers. Add the ramps, salt, and pepper and cook, turning the ramps frequently, for 1 to 2 minutes. Reduce the heat to medium-low, add the butter, and cook, stirring occasionally, until the ramps are tender, about 20 minutes more.

pan-roasted spring onions

The first spring shoots of the onion have a fresher, greener flavor than regular onions, which are left to cure once they are pulled, causing a papery skin and stronger flavors to develop.

12 spring onions	Freshly ground black pepper
1 to 2 tablespoons peanut oil	1 tablespoon unsalted butter
Kosher salt	

1. Clean and trim the onions, peeling off any bruised outer layers and cutting all but about 2 inches of the green shoot.

2. Heat the oil in a large skillet over medium heat until it moves easily across the pan. Add the spring onions and salt and pepper. Cook, turning every few minutes, until the onions begin to soften, about 5 minutes. Add the butter, reduce the heat to medium-low, and cook, turning the onions frequently, until they are tender and golden, about 3 minutes more.

rhubarb chutney

Rhubarb is a distant sharp relative of celery. Despite its popularity in pies, I feel it pairs better with savory foods than sweet. The sugar in this recipe helps to balance the tartness of the fruit. Rhubarb chutney makes a great accompaniment to foie gras, squab, and duck.

1 tablespoon peanut oil
1 small onion, peeled, halved, and thinly sliced
Kosher salt and freshly ground black pepper
4 rhubarb stalks, peeled and sliced about 1 inch thick

1 tablespoon grated fresh ginger
3 garlic cloves, peeled and sliced
1 bay leaf
About 2 tablespoons sugar
¼ cup cider vinegar
2 tablespoons chopped chives (optional)

Heat the oil over medium-low heat in a medium saucepan until it thins slightly. Add the onion, salt, and pepper and cook, stirring occasionally, until soft, about 15 minutes. Add the rhubarb, ginger, garlic, and bay leaf and cook, stirring occasionally, until the rhubarb begins to soften, about 10 minutes. Add the sugar and vinegar and cook until the rhubarb is completely soft and the chutney is the consistency of chunky applesauce, about 7 minutes more. Adjust the seasoning with sugar, salt, and pepper. Serve warm or at room temperature topped with chopped chives. The chutney will keep in the refrigerator for several weeks.

fava bean and pecorino salad with prosciutto

SERVES 4

Here I've taken the basic component, fava beans, and layered it with sheep's-milk cheese and prosciutto into a more evolved dish. If pecorino is unavailable, use any sharp (preferably sheep's-milk) cheese you can find.

Kosher salt
1½ pounds fava beans, shelled
5 tablespoons chopped walnuts
2½ tablespoons walnut oil (or olive oil)
Freshly ground black pepper
7 large radishes, trimmed

2 teaspoons chopped fresh sage
1 tablespoon chopped fresh chives
¼ pound thinly sliced prosciutto
2 tablespoons extra-virgin olive oil
1 lemon, quartered
1 small piece Pecorino Romano

1. Bring a large pot of salted water to a boil over high heat. Cook the fava beans in the water until they are tender and can be easily peeled, about 5 minutes. Drain the beans, rinse them under cold water, then slip off the tough outer skins (see sidenote). Place the favas in a bowl.

The easiest way to peel a fava bean is to tear off one tip of the casing, then pinch on the other end gently until the bean slides out. Unlike other beans, which benefit from slow cooking, favas should be treated as a green vegetable—cooked quickly in salted boiling water.

2. Combine the walnuts and walnut oil in a food processor and pulse until you have a coarse paste. Season the walnut paste with salt and pepper.

3. Thinly slice the radishes. Add the radishes, sage, chives, walnut paste, salt, and pepper to the fava beans and mix well.

4. Divide the prosciutto among 4 plates, top with fava bean salad, and drizzle with olive oil. Squeeze a little lemon juice over each salad, top each salad with thinly shaved Pecorino, and serve.

For the photograph, we garnished the salad with pepato, a peppered Pecorino from Sicily.

swiss chard cannelloni with chanterelle sauce

This dish is yet another example of how foods of the same season marry well; the earthiness of the Swiss chard works nicely against the piney flavor of chanterelles. For information on buying or ordering chanterelles, see page 266.

FOR THE CHANTERELLE SAUCE
1 tablespoon peanut oil
1 shallot, peeled and minced
1 garlic clove, peeled and minced
½ pound chanterelle mushrooms, cleaned and trimmed (page 148)
Kosher salt and freshly ground black pepper
1½ to 2 cups White Chicken Stock (page 69)
1 sprig of fresh thyme

FOR THE CANNELLONI
2 pounds Swiss chard
3 tablespoons peanut oil
1 leek, white part only, trimmed and chopped
1 garlic clove, peeled and chopped
Kosher salt and freshly ground black pepper
8 (8½-inch) crepes (page 180)
1 tablespoon unsalted butter
8 spring onions, green part trimmed and halved lengthwise

1. **Making the sauce.** Heat the oil in a deep skillet over medium heat until it moves easily across the pan. Add the shallot and garlic. Cook, stirring frequently, until the shallot begins to soften, about 3 minutes.

2. Reserve 8 small chanterelles for garnish. Add the remaining mushrooms to the skillet. Add salt and pepper and cook, stirring frequently, until the mushrooms soften slightly, about 5 minutes. Add 1½ cups of the stock and the thyme and simmer until the mushrooms are very tender, 5 to 10 minutes.

3. Purée the mushroom mixture in a blender until smooth. Add up to ½ cup stock if the sauce is too thick—the sauce should be just thick enough to nap a wooden spoon. Taste for salt and pepper and set the sauce aside.

4. **Making the cannelloni.** Cut the Swiss chard leaves from the stalks, discarding all but 4 of the stalks. Heat 1 tablespoon of the oil in a large skillet over medium heat

until it slides easily across the pan. Add the leek and garlic and cook until the leek begins to soften, about 3 minutes. Add the Swiss chard leaves a handful at a time, seasoning with salt and pepper. Let the chard wilt a bit before adding the next handful. Cook, stirring frequently, until the chard is wilted and tender, about 10 minutes. Transfer the chard mixture to a colander. Drain thoroughly, squeeze dry, then chop.

5. Trim the crepes into even circles, fill each crepe with chard mixture, then roll tightly.

6. **Assembling the dish.** Heat the oven to 250°F. Heat 1 tablespoon of the oil in a large skillet over medium heat until it slides easily across the pan. Place the cannelloni in the skillet, seam-side down. Add the butter and cook, turning to brown on all sides, about 3 minutes. Keep the cannelloni warm in the oven.

7. Cut the reserved chard stalks into 2-inch lengths. Heat the remaining tablespoon of oil in a small skillet over medium heat until it slides. Add the chard stalks, spring onions, salt, and pepper and cook, turning once or twice, until the stalks begin to soften, 1 to 3 minutes. Add the reserved chanterelles and cook until the vegetables are tender and golden, about 10 minutes.

8. Meanwhile, warm the chanterelle sauce over low heat. Divide the sauce among 4 plates, place 2 cannelloni on each plate, and garnish with the spring onions, chanterelles, and chard mixture.

pan-roasted asparagus

SERVES 4

This is a great example of how using an unexpected technique can completely alter the nuance of a dish. Blanching or steaming asparagus will give you a pure, fresh asparagus flavor, but cooking it this way instead allows woodier, roasted flavors to emerge that one normally does not associate with asparagus.

2 tablespoons peanut oil
2 pounds thin asparagus, trimmed
Kosher salt and freshly ground black pepper

About 3 tablespoons unsalted butter
1 teaspoon fresh thyme leaves
Coarse sea salt (optional)

1. Place the oil in a large skillet and heat over medium-high heat until it shimmers. Add the asparagus, a handful at a time, making sure the pan is always sizzling but never smoking.

2. Add kosher salt and pepper and reduce the heat to medium. Cook the asparagus, turning the stalks occasionally. When the pan begins to look dry, begin adding the butter a tablespoon at a time.

If you are using thin, pencil asparagus, simply break off the bottoms and peel off any small leaves. For thicker asparagus, you will need to trim the tough ends and peel the woody stems, just as you would a carrot. Thicker asparagus will take longer to cook, so adjust the cooking time accordingly.

3. Cook the asparagus, continuing to turn the stalks, for about 10 minutes. Add the thyme and a little more salt and cook until the asparagus is tender, about 5 minutes more. Serve immediately sprinkled with sea salt if desired.

summer
vegetables

L**IKE LOTS OF KIDS FROM** N**EW** J**ERSEY,** I **SPENT MY SUMMERS** "**DOWN** the shore." We escaped the heat on the craggy beaches that stud the coastline of southern New Jersey, in towns like Belmar and Bradley Beach, and it was there that I grew my hair long as a teenager, listened to Springsteen, and did things I can't print here.

But it wasn't until I started to cook that I began to appreciate what summer really means: It's a season of riches. In the greenmarket, tables are heaped high with verdant peas, majestic favas, and wild young greens. Bundles of fresh herbs, their leaves a tangle of fragrance and tiny blossoms, beckon cooks away from winter's heavier spices. An embarrassment of fruit—peaches, plums, berries—assaults my senses, and I buy them all, afraid to see any go to waste.

As the days continue to lengthen, hardier vegetables appear with such plenitude you can't give them away. Like zucchini and summer squash. Corn so sweet it tastes like dessert. Basil, growing like the weed it is, leaves its heady scent in the air and on the fingers of those who touch as they buy. And, of course, summer brings tomatoes—although I think that here in the Northeast, tomatoes really reach their peak as summer gives way to early fall.

The beauty of summer is how little intervention the food needs to show itself. The vegetables of summer are blessed with water and sugars in abundance, and it is hard to improve upon them. I love simple cooking in the summer—foods lightly dressed and tossed on the grill, simple roasted fish and meats. As the father of a seven-year-old, I prefer to spend these long days fishing or splashing in the surf, and not behind a stove.

summer vegetable ragout

This recipe is a two-step process: First blanch the vegetables separately *just* to the point of being done, then reheat them all together in a little beurre fondue. Taste as you go: A properly cooked vegetable will have much more flavor than one that is undercooked. (See my note about undercooked vegetables, page 66.)

FOR THE VEGETABLES (choose at least 4 varieties; you will need 4 to 6 cups of cut vegetables in all)
Fresh cranberry beans, shelled
Fresh garbanzo beans
Green beans
Broad beans
Wax beans
Peas
Bok choy
Swiss chard (leaves and stems cooked separately)
Celery
Shallots
Leeks (white part only)
Zucchini
Yellow squash
Pattypan squash
Carrots

Kosher salt

FOR THE BEURRE FONDUE
½ cup (1 stick) unsalted butter, chilled and cut into pieces

FOR THE RAGOUT
1 small piece of Duck Ham (page 185) or prosciutto, cut into 4 pieces (optional)
1 to 2 tablespoons mixed chopped fresh herbs (such as tarragon, chervil, thyme, flat-leaf parsley, and chives)
Kosher salt and freshly ground black pepper
4 cherry tomatoes, halved
2 radishes, thinly sliced
¼ cup vegetable sprouts (such as broccoli, radish, or alfalfa)

1. Preparing the vegetables. Clean, trim, then cut each vegetable so each type is consistently cut but not necessarily cut the same size as any other vegetable.

2. Cook each vegetable separately in boiling salted water until tender, refresh in cold water, then drain thoroughly. Combine the vegetables in a large bowl once they are cooked.

3. Making the beurre fondue. Bring about ½ inch of water to a boil in a small saucepan. Reduce the heat to medium-low and whisk in the butter one piece at a time. (For more about making beurre fondue, see page 77). Transfer to a medium saucepan.

4. Finishing the ragout. Adjust the heat to maintain a low simmer. Add the duck ham or prosciutto (if using), then add the vegetables, gently mixing and coating with beurre fondue. Add the herbs, salt, pepper, cherry tomatoes, and radishes and gently simmer until the vegetables are just heated through. Divide the duck ham and vegetables among 4 plates or shallow bowls, garnish with sprouts, and serve.

ratatouille

4 small zucchini
1 small eggplant
3 red bell peppers, cored and seeded
1 green bell pepper, cored and seeded
2 tomatoes, halved and seeded
½ cup extra-virgin olive oil

1 onion, peeled and chopped
Kosher salt and freshly ground black
    pepper
5 garlic cloves, peeled and sliced
6 sprigs of fresh basil

1. Split the zucchini lengthwise, then slice into thin half-moons. Cut the eggplant lengthwise into 6 pieces, then slice. Slice the red and green peppers thin. Cut the tomato halves in half again and cut into thin lengths.

2. Heat about 2 tablespoons of the oil in a large, heavy skillet over medium-high heat until it shimmers. Add the onion, salt, and pepper and cook, stirring frequently, until the onion is tender and golden, about 10 minutes. Transfer to a large bowl, wipe out the skillet, and add another tablespoon of oil.

3. Working in batches if necessary, cook the zucchini until they begin to soften, about 3 minutes. Add a little garlic, a sprig of basil, and salt and pepper and continue cooking until the zucchini are almost tender, 2 to 3 minutes more. Add the zucchini to the onion, then wipe out the skillet. Cook the eggplant, again in batches if necessary, adding more oil, and adding garlic, basil, salt, and pepper when the eggplant is about half-cooked. Add the eggplant to the onion.

4. Repeat, wiping out the pan and cooking the peppers and flavoring them with garlic and basil. When the peppers are almost done, 3 to 5 minutes, add the tomatoes to the skillet. Cook the mixture until the tomatoes release their juices, 3 to 5 minutes more, then add the onion, zucchini, and eggplant mixture. Reduce the heat to medium-low and gently simmer the ratatouille, partially covered, until all the vegetables are tender, about 15 minutes more.

5. Spoon the ratatouille into a colander set over a bowl. Let the vegetables drain for a few minutes, then pour the juices into a small pan. Reduce the vegetable juices over high heat until they thicken slightly. Combine the reduced juices and the drained ratatouille in the skillet. Warm over low heat and serve.

eggplant caviar

This is delicious as a spread on crusty bread, or alongside roasted or braised fish.

2 medium eggplants
4 to 5 tablespoons extra-virgin olive oil
Kosher salt and freshly ground black
   pepper

3 garlic cloves, unpeeled
1 red bell pepper
¼ pound shiitake mushrooms, stemmed
   and sliced

1. Heat the oven to 500° F. Slice the eggplants in half lengthwise, then, without cutting the skins, score the flesh in a crosshatch pattern. Sprinkle the eggplants with about 1 tablespoon of the olive oil and with salt and pepper and place, cut-side up, on a cookie sheet. Wrap the garlic in aluminum foil and place on the same cookie sheet. Cover the eggplants with aluminum foil and roast for 25 minutes. Remove the foil from the eggplants and check the garlic. If the garlic is soft, remove it from the oven, otherwise continue roasting both the wrapped garlic and the uncovered eggplants. The eggplant is done when it is soft and golden, about 30 minutes more.

2. Char the pepper over an open-burner flame, then place it in a sealed bag or plastic container until cool enough to handle. Gently scrape away the charred skin, discard the stem and seeds, and cut out the veins. Dice the pepper and set aside.

3. Heat 2 tablespoons of the oil in a large skillet over medium heat until it slides easily across the pan. Add the mushrooms, salt, and pepper and sauté until the mushrooms are browned and tender, about 5 minutes. Dice them and set them aside.

4. Scrape the eggplant pulp into a large bowl, discarding the skins. Add about 2 tablespoons of oil and whip the mixture with a fork until it is smooth. Squeeze the garlic out of its skin and add it to the eggplant with the diced pepper, mushrooms, salt, and pepper. Mix thoroughly and serve warm or at room temperature. The caviar will keep in the refrigerator for about 3 days.

pan-fried eggplant

MAKES 8 TO 10 SLICES

This dish is delicious alone, but I particularly like to layer the slices of eggplant with a dollop of Eggplant Caviar (page 209) to form an eggplant "napoleon," which I serve with Lemon–Rosemary Vinaigrette (page 83).

1 egg	1 eggplant, thinly sliced
About 1 cup flour	3 to 6 tablespoons peanut oil
About 1 cup dried unseasoned bread crumbs	Kosher salt

Beat the egg with 1 teaspoon water in a medium bowl. Place the flour and bread crumbs on separate plates. Working in batches, dip the eggplant slices first in flour, then egg, and then bread crumbs, shaking off any excess. Heat about ½ inch of oil over medium heat in a large skillet. Add only as many slices of eggplant as will fit comfortably in a single layer in the skillet. Season with salt. Cook the eggplant slices until they begin to brown, about 2 minutes, then turn the slices over and continue cooking for 1 to 2 minutes more. Drain on paper towels, wipe out the skillet, and repeat breading and frying the remaining eggplant.

Opposite: Eggplant "napoleon," with Braised Snapper (recipe, page 60) and Lemon–Rosemary Vinaigrette (recipe, page 83).

corn relish

I came up with this dish when I was looking for a way to serve cold corn with seared foie gras. It works equally well with grilled or roasted meats and fish.

6 ears of corn, shucked
1½ cups white wine vinegar
¼ cup sugar
1 garlic clove, peeled and minced
1 tablespoon grated fresh ginger
1 sprig of fresh tarragon
1 sprig of fresh thyme
1 tablespoon peanut oil

1 small yellow onion, peeled and diced
½ or 1 small jalapeño, seeded and
  minced
1 red bell pepper, seeded and diced
Kosher salt
5 scallions, white parts only, chopped
Cayenne pepper (optional)

1. Remove the kernels from the corn. Reserve the kernels and discard the cobs.

2. Combine the vinegar and sugar in a small saucepan and bring to a boil. Reduce the heat to medium and add the garlic and ginger and simmer until the vinegar mixture is reduced by about one-third, about 10 minutes. Remove the pot from the heat and add the tarragon and thyme. Allow the mixture to steep for about 5 minutes.

3. Heat the oil in a large saucepan over medium heat until it slides easily across the pan. Add the onion, jalapeño, and bell pepper. Season with salt and cook, stirring occasionally, until the pepper begins to soften, 1 to 2 minutes. Add the corn, scallions, cayenne (if using), and salt. Cook, stirring, until the corn turns bright yellow, about 2 minutes more. Add the vinegar mixture to the corn mixture and bring to a simmer. Reduce the heat to medium-low and cook just until the corn is tender, about 5 minutes. Refrigerate for at least 1 day before serving. The relish should be stored in the refrigerator, where it will last several weeks.

corn chowder

If your guests ask how they can help, set them to chopping vegetables. Once everything is diced, this recipe is very simple. I like to serve the chowder topped with fried oysters (page 255).

5 ears of corn, shucked
2 cups heavy cream
1 red bell pepper
¼ pound slab bacon cut into thin strips
1 onion, peeled and chopped
4 small leeks, white part only, trimmed, halved lengthwise, and thinly sliced
1 garlic clove, peeled and sliced
1 bunch of scallions, whites only, chopped
4 celery stalks, peeled and diced

Kosher salt and freshly ground black pepper
1 cup chopped chanterelle mushrooms (optional)
4 russet or all-purpose potatoes (about 3½ pounds), peeled and diced
¼ teaspoon caraway seed
1 small jalapeño pepper, seeded and minced
1 sprig of fresh tarragon
2 cups White Chicken Stock (page 69)
Chopped fresh chives (optional)

1. Remove the kernels from the corn and reserve. Steep the cobs, uncovered, in the cream in a deep saucepan over very low heat (the cream should steam but not simmer) for about 10 minutes. Turn off the heat, but leave the cobs in the cream.

2. Char the pepper over an open-burner flame, then place in a sealed bag or plastic container until cool enough to handle. Gently scrape away the charred skin, discard the stem and seeds, and cut out the veins. Dice the pepper and set aside.

3. Cook the bacon over medium-low heat in a large soup pot until the fat is rendered but the bacon not yet crisp, about 2 minutes.

4. Add the onion, leeks, and garlic and cook, stirring frequently, until the vegetables begin to soften, about 10 minutes. Add the scallions, celery, and salt and pepper, cook for 3 to 4 minutes, then add the chanterelles (if using). When the celery is almost tender add the potatoes and cook, stirring occasionally, until the potatoes begin to release starch, about 5 minutes. Add the caraway seed, jalapeño,

diced roasted pepper, and tarragon, and cook for 1 minute more. Stir in the reserved corn.

5. Add the chicken stock a little at a time (keep the chowder at a constant gentle simmer). Strain the cream and stir it into the chowder. Taste for salt and pepper and simmer gently until the potatoes are tender, about 20 minutes. Serve garnished with chopped chives if desired.

creamless creamed corn

In experimenting with different vegetable juices one day, I discovered that heating corn "juice" caused it to thicken quickly, due to the natural cornstarch. This led to a modern interpretation of the creamed corn I loved as a kid, and is a good example of how experimenting with an ingredient can yield discoveries that change the way you cook.

12 ears of corn, shucked
Kosher salt and freshly ground black
   pepper

2 tablespoons unsalted butter (optional)

1. Using a box grater, grate the kernels from 5 ears of corn into a bowl. Press the grated corn through a fine sieve, reserving the "milk" and discarding the grated corn and the cobs.

2. Cut the kernels from the remaining ears of corn. Combine the corn kernels, ¼ cup water, salt, and pepper in a medium pan. Cover the pan and steam over medium-low heat, stirring once or twice, until the corn is tender, about 5 minutes. Drain, then set the corn aside.

3. Stirring constantly, bring the corn "milk" to a simmer over medium heat in a medium saucepan. Reduce the heat to medium-low and cook, continuing to stir, until the "milk" thickens, about 3 minutes. Add the cooked corn, salt, pepper, and butter (if using) and cook until the corn is heated through. Serve warm.

Certain varieties of corn are being grown (in Florida, for example) that are labeled "super sweet." I'm not a big fan; the extra sugar makes dishes come out too sweet and it lacks the starch that will cause the "creamed" corn to thicken. Locally grown corn bought in season will be sweet enough, and better than anything shipped from a distance.

corn and potato pancakes

I like to juxtapose a homey comfort food like these pancakes with a luxury food like caviar.

1 large Idaho or other russet potato
   (about ¾ pound), scrubbed
2 eggs, separated, plus 2 egg whites
1½ tablespoons flour
1½ tablespoons crème fraîche
2 cups corn kernels (from about 2 ears)

Kosher salt and freshly ground black
   pepper
1 tablespoon peanut oil
1 to 2 tablespoons unsalted butter
   (optional)

1. Heat the oven to 400° F. Bake the potato until tender, about 1 hour and 15 minutes. When the potato is cool enough to handle, peel and mash. Set aside in a large bowl. Reduce the oven temperature to 250° F.

2. Lightly beat the egg yolks. Add the flour and crème fraîche and mix well. Add the potato, corn, salt, and pepper. Beat the 4 egg whites until they form soft peaks, then gently fold the egg whites into the corn and potato batter.

3. Heat a large skillet over medium-low. Add just enough oil to coat the pan. Form several pancakes, dropping the batter into the pan a tablespoon at a time, then flattening and shaping each pancake with the back of the spoon. Cook the pancakes until they begin to bubble around the edges and the bottoms are golden, 1 to 3 minutes. Turn the pancakes and cook about 2 minutes more. Add a little bit of butter to the pan (if using), turn the pancakes in the melting butter, then transfer them to the warm oven. Repeat, forming and cooking the remaining pancakes.

zucchini with lemon thyme

Lemon thyme is available in greenmarkets, in season only. If you can, I recommend planting a little of it for yourself. I did just that on my windowsill here in New York City and the combination of pollution and benign neglect hasn't kept it from growing like a weed and lending its subtle lemony flavor to my food when I need it. If you have difficulty finding the herb, substitute fresh thyme, and use a little more lemon zest instead.

3 tablespoons extra-virgin olive oil
6 small zucchini, thinly sliced
Kosher salt and freshly ground black
   pepper

1 or 2 sprigs of fresh lemon thyme
1 teaspoon chopped lemon zest
12 Niçoise olives, pitted (optional)

1. Heat 2 tablespoons of the oil in a large skillet over medium heat until it moves easily across the pan. Add the zucchini and salt and pepper and cook, turning once or twice, until the zucchini begin to soften, about 5 minutes, then add the lemon thyme. Gradually add enough water to barely cover the bottom of the skillet, 3 to 5 tablespoons, a tablespoon at a time, bringing the pot to a simmer before each addition.

2. Gently simmer the zucchini until they are cooked through, about 5 minutes more, then add the lemon zest, the remaining tablespoon of olive oil, and the olives (if using). Taste for salt and pepper and serve.

pan-roasted zucchini

SERVES 4

I like this dish better than fried zucchini; roasting slowly allows the flavor of the zucchini to develop.

2 to 4 tablespoons extra-virgin olive oil
6 small zucchini, sliced

Kosher salt and freshly ground black pepper

1. Heat 2 tablespoons of the oil in a large skillet over medium heat until it slides easily across the pan. Working in batches, cook the zucchini in a single layer until they begin to soften, 3 to 5 minutes. Reduce the heat to medium-low, add salt and pepper, and continue cooking until the zucchini are browned, about 5 minutes. Turn them and cook until the second sides brown and the zucchini are tender, about 5 minutes more. Transfer the first batch to a plate and repeat with the remaining zucchini, adding more oil if needed.

2. When all the zucchini have been cooked, return them to the skillet and reheat over medium heat. Serve immediately.

pan-fried zucchini blossoms

Zucchini blossoms may be hard to find because they are very perishable. I recommend asking around at your local greenmarket. I like to serve these as a garnish for Zucchini with Lemon Thyme (page 218), but they also make a great stand-alone hors d'oeuvre. Dante's friend Charlotte, age six, particularly loves them as a snack.

8 zucchini blossoms

2 eggs

¾ cup superfine or all-purpose flour

2 tablespoons extra-virgin olive oil

Kosher salt and freshly ground black pepper

1. Trim off the base of each zucchini blossom. Discard each base and center, then cut the blossoms so they lie flat.

2. Beat the eggs with 2 teaspoons water in a small bowl. Divide the flour between 2 more bowls. Heat the oil in a large skillet over medium heat until it slides easily across the pan. Dredge the blossoms first in flour, then egg, then flour again, shaking off any excess. Fry the blossoms just until crisp, 1 to 2 minutes per side, then drain on paper towels. Season with salt and pepper and serve as an appetizer or a garnish for Zucchini with Lemon Thyme.

pickled watermelon rind

I created this version on the spot the day I got a call from a *New York Times* editor who was writing a piece on watermelons used in savory cooking. I paired the pickled watermelon with rabbit, but you can use it to garnish almost any summertime meat or fish. I haven't given a yield here because it varies so much depending on the size of the watermelon and whether you opt for cubes or lengths.

1 tablespoon black peppercorns
1 tablespoon mustard seed
1 tablespoon coriander seed
1 tablespoon fennel seed
1 tablespoon cardamom seed

¼ cup sugar
2 garlic cloves, peeled
3 cups white wine vinegar
Rind from half a watermelon, cut into
    lengths or cubes

Combine the peppercorns, mustard, coriander, fennel, cardamom, sugar, garlic, and vinegar with 2 cups water in a nonreactive saucepan and bring to a boil. Place the watermelon rinds in a large jar or bowl. Pour the boiling pickling liquid over the rinds, cover, and refrigerate for at least 2 weeks before serving. Store the pickled watermelon rind in the refrigerator, where it will last several weeks.

tomato consommé

This dish was a happy accident: After dicing a batch of tomatoes I noticed an intense tomato water had collected in the bowl. It tasted great, but looked awful, so I heated it up, causing the solids to fall away and leaving a clear broth with a concentrated tomato flavor. Slice some ripe tomatoes into the consommé and serve it cold, finished with olive oil and coarse salt, for a refreshing appetizer.

10 large ripe (or overripe) tomatoes	Kosher salt

1. Working in batches, pulse the tomatoes in a blender or food processor.

2. Set a fine sieve over a bowl. Line the sieve with a large double layer of cheesecloth. Place about a cup of the tomato purée in the sieve and sprinkle with salt. Repeat until you have transferred and salted all of the purée. Wrap the cheesecloth around the tomatoes, squeeze once or twice, then place the bowl, sieve, and tomatoes in the refrigerator for 24 hours to drip.

3. Squeeze the tomato pulp one more time, then discard it. Place the tomato juice in a small saucepan and bring just to a simmer over medium heat, taking care never to allow the consommé to boil. Reduce the heat to medium-low and carefully skim off the solids as they rise to the surface.

4. Allow the consommé to cool completely. Set the sieve over a bowl and line it with fresh cheesecloth. Ladle the consommé through the sieve, leaving any solids in the bottom of the pan.

5. To serve, chill the consommé or reheat it very gently over low heat and serve warm. The consommé will keep in the refrigerator for 3 to 5 days.

green tomato chutney

At the end of the tomato season, there are usually a bunch of unripe tomatoes left over on the vine. Their firmness makes them a great ingredient for chutney, as they'll hold their shape nicely throughout cooking.

1 tablespoon peanut oil
1 garlic clove, peeled and minced
2 jalapeño peppers, seeded and minced
1 tablespoon minced fresh ginger
3 shallots, peeled and minced
1 red bell pepper, cored, seeded, and cut into small dice
10 green tomatoes, peeled, seeded, and cut into small dice
Kosher salt

2 green cardamom pods
½ teaspoon mustard seed
½ teaspoon dried mustard
½ teaspoon coriander seed
½ teaspoon fennel seed
¼ teaspoon cayenne pepper
1 cup white wine vinegar
2 tablespoons sugar
1 sprig of fresh tarragon
1 sprig of fresh thyme

Heat the oil in a large saucepan over medium heat until it slides easily across the pan. Add the garlic, jalapeños, ginger, shallots, and bell pepper. Cook, stirring frequently, for 1 to 2 minutes, then add the green tomatoes and salt. Cook, stirring frequently, for about 2 minutes more, then add the cardamom, mustard seed, dried mustard, coriander seed, fennel seed, and cayenne. When the spices are fragrant, 1 to 2 minutes more, add the vinegar, sugar, tarragon, and thyme. Reduce the heat to low and cook at a gentle simmer until the tomatoes are tender, about 30 minutes. Adjust the seasoning with salt, sugar, and cayenne and serve warm, cool, or at room temperature. This chutney should be stored in the refrigerator, where it will last several weeks.

pepper chutney

My co-chef at 40 Main Street, Jerry Bryan, came up with this great garnish as a way to use up extra peppers. I like a mix of varieties to add some complexity, but feel free to use whichever peppers are abundant and look good. Bell peppers alone will give you a milder chutney.

½ cup golden raisins

12 red bell peppers, cored and seeded

2 yellow bell peppers, cored and seeded

1 sweet long green Italian pepper, cored
   and seeded

2 tablespoons peanut oil

1 onion, peeled and finely chopped

1½ tablespoons minced fresh ginger

3 garlic cloves, peeled and minced

2 jalapeño peppers, seeded and minced

Kosher salt

½ teaspoon ground mace

½ teaspoon dried mustard

1 teaspoon mustard seed

2 tablespoons sugar

1 tablespoon tomato paste

1 cup white wine vinegar

1. Place the raisins in a small bowl, cover with very hot water, and set aside for at least 30 minutes to plump, replacing the hot water once or twice.

2. Remove the soft white ribs from the red, yellow, and green peppers, then cut them all into a small dice.

3. Heat the oil in a large skillet over medium-low until it thins slightly. Add the onion and cook, stirring occasionally, until the onion softens, about 15 minutes. Add the ginger and garlic and cook until the mixture is fragrant, about 3 minutes, then add the diced peppers, jalapeños, and salt. Cook, stirring occasionally, until the peppers soften and release their juices, about 15 minutes, then stir in the mace, dried mustard, and mustard seed. Cook for about a minute, then add the sugar, tomato paste, and vinegar. Continue cooking until the peppers are very tender and the chutney is thick, about 15 minutes. Drain the raisins and add them to the chutney and gently simmer for about 10 minutes more. Allow the chutney to cool, then refrigerate until ready to use. This chutney should be stored in the refrigerator, where it will last several weeks.

fall vegetables

I N MY EARLY TWENTIES, I SPENT AN ENTIRE AUTUMN COOKING IN France, and it changed forever the way I viewed the season. Fall no longer marked the close of summer's rich bounty; rather it was the start of something entirely its own.

In autumn vegetables, the high notes of color and intensity settle into a bass line of starchier, sturdier varieties. To an extent, this reflects plants getting ready for winter, and our cooking reflects the same change as we prepare for the colder months. The flavors become mellow and darker, the textures get denser and richer, and in many ways, we have to do more with the ingredients to coax out their flavor.

Slower cooking of fall vegetables gives us a chance to introduce new flavors into a dish.

Mostly, the cooking process slows down. In summer, it takes mere minutes to cook corn, but as winter rolls around we need to spend a little extra time roasting endive or glazing onions. Slower cooking does, however, give us a chance to introduce new flavors into a dish. Braised red cabbage is a perfect example: Braising the vegetable in red wine slowly infuses it with a richness and redolence it wouldn't ordinarily have. Slow cooking, like glazing an endive or roasting root vegetables, draws out the sugars and transforms the vegetable into something lush and comforting, which is well suited to autumn.

Pan-Roasted Striped Bass (recipe, page 39)
with Braised Red Cabbage.

braised red cabbage

The color of the cabbage makes this dish especially beautiful on the plate. Mixing wine and wine vinegar keeps the acidity of the braising liquid in check.

4 small or 2 large heads of red cabbage, trimmed, quartered, and cored
1 tablespoon peanut oil
Kosher salt and freshly ground black pepper

1 teaspoon caraway seed
1 cup dry red wine
⅓ cup red wine vinegar
3 tablespoons sugar

1. Separate the leaves of cabbage. Cut away and discard the tough ribs, then cut the cabbage leaves into thin strips.

2. Heat the oil in a medium saucepan over medium heat until the oil slides easily across the pan. Add a little of the cabbage and salt and pepper. Cook, stirring, until the cabbage wilts, then add a little more. Continue cooking, adding, seasoning, and stirring until all the cabbage is wilted. Add the caraway seed and cook, stirring, for about 1 minute. Add the wine and vinegar and bring to a simmer. Sprinkle the sugar over the cabbage and mix well.

3. Reduce the heat to medium-low, partially cover, and gently simmer, stirring occasionally, until most of the liquid has evaporated and the cabbage is soft and shiny, about 45 minutes. Remove the cabbage from the heat and allow to stand for 5 minutes. Serve warm or at room temperature.

roasted savoy cabbage with raisins

SERVES 4

It might seem odd to roast a leaf vegetable, but the density of cabbage makes this dish work. Roast cabbage just as you would a piece of meat: Brown it first, use a medium heat, and finish with a small amount of butter.

2 tablespoons golden raisins
1 large head of Savoy cabbage, trimmed, quartered, and cored
2 tablespoons peanut oil
1 leek, white part only, trimmed and thinly sliced
1 medium carrot, peeled and thinly sliced

2 medium parsnips, peeled and thinly sliced
1 medium white turnip, peeled, quartered, and thinly sliced
Kosher salt and freshly ground black pepper
3 tablespoons unsalted butter
2 sprigs of fresh thyme

1. Place the raisins in a small bowl, cover with very hot water, and set aside for at least 30 minutes to plump, replacing the hot water once or twice. Tear all the cabbage into large pieces.

2. Heat the oven to 400° F. Heat the oil in a large ovenproof skillet over medium heat until it slides easily across the pan. Add the leek, carrot, parsnips, turnip, salt, and pepper. Cook, stirring often, until the leek begins to soften, about 5 minutes. Add a little cabbage, salt, and pepper and cook, stirring. When the cabbage begins to soften add more, continuing until all the cabbage has been added. Add the butter, thyme, and a little more salt and pepper. Cook, turning the vegetables in the melting butter, until all the cabbage has wilted, about 3 minutes more. Drain the raisins and stir them into the cabbage mixture.

3. Transfer the skillet to the oven and roast, stirring every 10 minutes or so, until the cabbage is tender, about 40 minutes. Serve immediately.

roasted endive with whole spices

In my kitchen is a box of whole Indian spices, which my fiancée received as a gift. I liked the way the "whole" seeds adhered to the endive; the effect was better than ground spices would have been. I used most of the seeds in the box, but you should experiment with whichever whole spices you have available.

8 heads of endive

1 tablespoon peanut oil

Kosher salt and freshly ground black
    pepper

1 tablespoon unsalted butter

6 green cardamom pods

½ teaspoon mustard seed

¼ teaspoon cumin seed

¼ teaspoon coriander seed

¼ teaspoon fennel seed

¼ teaspoon fenugreek

1. Heat the oven to 350° F. Remove the large outer leaves from the endives, revealing the compact centers. Reserve the outer leaves for use elsewhere (see sidenote).

Save the outer leaves of the endives for Endive Chutney (page 234) or Glazed Endive Leaves (page 232).

2. Heat the oil in a large ovenproof skillet over medium heat until it slides easily across the pan. Add the endive hearts, salt, and pepper and cook, browning on all sides, about 5 minutes.

3. Transfer the endives to the oven and roast for about 10 minutes, then add the butter; cardamom; mustard, cumin, coriander, and fennel seeds; and fenugreek. Turn the endives over once or twice in the melting butter and return to the oven. Continue to roast, turning the endives from time to time, until each head is well browned and very tender, about 1 hour. Serve warm.

glazed endive leaves

Once the sugar is in the pan, watch carefully that it doesn't burn. If it starts to go past caramel, take the pan off the heat until it cools down. Add the vinegar and then continue to cook.

4 heads of endive

2 tablespoons peanut oil

Kosher salt and freshly ground black pepper

1 teaspoon sugar

1 tablespoon unsalted butter

1½ teaspoons balsamic vinegar

1. Discard any damaged endive leaves, then separate the large outer leaves. Reserve the centers for another purpose (see Roasted Endive with Whole Spices sidenote, page 231). Heat 1 tablespoon of the oil in a large skillet over medium-low heat until it thins slightly. Add half the endive leaves, bowed-side up, and cook, pressing down so the leaves brown evenly, about 3 minutes. Turn the leaves, add salt and pepper, and brown on the second side, about 3 minutes more.

To keep endives white, farmers mound soil over the bulbs as they sprout. This keeps them from photosynthesizing and acquiring tougher, green leaves.

2. Sprinkle the leaves with half the sugar and add half the butter. Turn the leaves as they cook in the browning butter and sugar. Cook for about a minute, then add ¾ teaspoon of the vinegar. Continue cooking, turning once or twice, until the endives are soft and coated with the balsamic glaze. Transfer the glazed leaves to a plate to cool. Wipe out the skillet and repeat, browning and then glazing the remaining endives.

3. Just before serving, warm the endives in the skillet over medium heat, adding more vinegar, salt, and pepper if necessary.

Opposite: Glazed Endive Leaves, Lentils (recipe, page 250), and Braised Fresh "Bacon" (recipe, page 58).

endive chutney

This chutney works especially well with hearty winter meats like venison or beef.

2 tablespoons golden raisins

1 leek, white part only, trimmed

4 heads of endive, trimmed

1 tablespoon peanut oil

1 shallot, peeled and thinly sliced

Kosher salt and freshly ground black
pepper

¾ tablespoon minced fresh ginger

1 garlic clove, peeled and minced

1 to 1½ tablespoons sugar

¼ cup white wine vinegar

¼ teaspoon coriander seed

¼ teaspoon mustard seed

1. Place the raisins in a small bowl, cover with very hot water, and set aside for at least 30 minutes to plump, replacing the hot water once or twice.

2. Cut the leek into 2-inch lengths and set aside. Discard the outer leaves from the endives. Separate the remaining leaves and cut them into lengths about the size of the leeks.

The vinegar in most chutneys acts as a preservative; this one will keep for about two weeks in the refrigerator. That is, unless you keep sticking a finger in there to taste — that will hasten the spoiling process.

3. Heat the oil in a medium skillet over medium heat until it slides easily across the pan. Add the leek, endives, shallot, salt, and pepper and cook, stirring frequently, until the vegetables begin to soften, about 5 minutes. Add the ginger and garlic and cook until fragrant, about 3 more minutes. Add 1 tablespoon of the sugar, the vinegar, and the coriander and mustard seeds. Drain the raisins and stir them into the chutney. Cook, stirring occasionally, until the pan is almost dry, about 20 minutes. Adjust the seasoning with salt, pepper, vinegar, and sugar and serve warm or at room temperature.

onion confit

Onion confit is an important component of many of my recipes; you'll see it used throughout this book in dishes like the Artichoke and Tomato Gratin (page 140) or the Caramelized Mushroom Tarts (page 122). It will last for weeks in the fridge, so make a batch and then use it down the road as the impetus for more ambitious dishes.

2 tablespoons extra-virgin olive oil
6 onions, peeled and thinly sliced (about 12 cups)
Kosher salt and freshly ground black pepper

1 cup White Chicken Stock (page 69)
2 tablespoons white wine vinegar
2 tablespoons fresh thyme leaves
4 anchovy fillets, chopped (optional)

Heat the oil in a large deep skillet over medium heat until it slides easily across the pan. Add the onions and salt and pepper. Reduce the heat to medium-low and cook, stirring occasionally, until the onions are very soft but not brown, about 30 minutes. Add the stock and vinegar and simmer, continuing to stir occasionally, until the pan is dry and the onions are golden, about 30 minutes more. Add the thyme leaves and anchovies (if using) and mix well. Serve warm or at room temperature. The confit should be refrigerated and will last at least a week.

honey-glazed onions

When chefs visit my restaurants they are always intrigued by these leaves of "stained glass" that adorn the plates. Although the recipe takes a bit of time, it is easy to do and leaves you with intensely caramelized onion petals that work wonderfully with sweetbreads or foie gras.

2 large onions, peeled
1 to 2 tablespoons peanut oil
Kosher salt and freshly ground black
    pepper

¼ cup honey
1 tablespoon unsalted butter

1. Cut the onions in half lengthwise through the root end. Cut each onion half lengthwise into thirds. Separate the outer layers from one another. Reserve the small centers for another use.

2. Heat the oil in a large skillet over medium heat until it slides easily across the pan. Add the onions, salt, and pepper and cook, stirring frequently and separating the onions into single "leaves." Cook the onions until they are soft and golden, and visibly deflated, about 30 minutes. Adjust the heat, if necessary, to prevent burning.

3. Add the honey and continue cooking until the honey begins to thicken, about 10 minutes, then stir in the butter. Cook the onions until they are almost completely dry, separating the leaves, about 25 minutes more.

4. Line cookie sheets with plastic wrap or parchment paper. Life out the onion leaves one by one, and air-dry them in a single layer, for about 20 minutes. Use immediately or store in an airtight container at room temperature for several weeks.

purée of onion soup

A soup like this can be easily refigured as a sauce by omitting the stock and adding just ¾ cup of water. The resulting onion soubise makes a creamy, flavorful accompaniment to roasted meat and fish or a delicious side dish by itself. The addition of olive oil and vinegar transforms it again into a creamy onion dressing.

2 tablespoons peanut oil
6 onions, peeled and sliced (about
   12 cups)
2 garlic cloves, peeled and sliced

Kosher salt and freshly ground black
   pepper
1 cup White Chicken Stock (page 69)
2 tablespoons unsalted butter

1. Heat the oil in a large saucepan over medium heat until it slides easily across the pan. Add the onions, garlic, salt, and pepper and cook, stirring occasionally, until the onions are soft, about 20 minutes.

2. Add the stock and 1 cup water and simmer for 10 minutes more. Purée the soup, then press it through a fine strainer.

3. Just before serving, reheat the soup, whisk in the butter, and add salt and pepper.

onion marmalade

This marmalade has a piquant sweet-and-sour quality. It is nice with grilled or roasted meat—especially liver.

2 tablespoons golden raisins

2 tablespoons peanut oil

4 onions, peeled and thinly sliced (about 8 cups)

Kosher salt and freshly ground black pepper

⅓ cup sugar

⅔ cup white wine vinegar

1 bay leaf

½ teaspoon coriander seed

3 green cardamom pods

1. Place the raisins in a small bowl, cover with very hot water, and set aside for at least 30 minutes to plump, replacing the hot water once or twice.

2. Heat the oil in a large, deep skillet over medium heat until it slides easily across the pan. Add the onions and season with salt and pepper. Reduce the heat to medium-low and cook, stirring occasionally, until the onions are very soft and dry but not brown, about 30 minutes.

3. Add the sugar and vinegar and simmer, continuing to stir occasionally, until the pan is dry and the onions are golden, about 30 minutes more. Drain the raisins and add them to the onions. Add the bay leaf, coriander seed, and cardamom, mix well, and cook, stirring frequently for 5 to 10 minutes more. Cool to room temperature and remove the bay leaf and serve. The marmalade should be refrigerated and will keep for several weeks.

balsamic onion marmalade

Since we opened Gramercy Tavern, I have served these balsamic onions in the front tavern room with filet mignon and mashed potatoes. Over the years, the dish has acquired cult status. I don't dare remove it from the menu.

1 tablespoon peanut oil
4 onions, peeled and thinly sliced (about 8 cups)
Kosher salt and freshly ground black pepper

⅓ cup sugar
⅔ cup balsamic vinegar

1. Heat the oil in a large skillet over medium heat until it slides easily across the pan. Add the onions, salt, and pepper and cook, stirring occasionally, until the onions are soft, about 20 minutes.

2. Add the sugar and reduce the heat to medium-low. Cook, stirring frequently, until the onions appear dry, about 10 minutes. Add the vinegar. Reduce the heat to low and cook, stirring occasionally, until the onions are soft and dry, about 1 hour. Serve warm or at room temperature. Store the marmalade in the refrigerator. It will keep for several weeks.

Balsamic vinegar gives this dish a haunting flavor, redolent of wooden casks and aged grapes. There is nothing else quite like it, and it is worth buying the best. Lesser-quality vinegars lack the nuance and intensity of true balsamic from Modena.

variation

Try adding some mace and clove or nutmeg as you cook down the onions, for a spiced marmalade.

potato, leek, and bacon pan-fry

SERVES 4

This recipe makes hash browns, only better. It works with everything, especially breakfast.

¼ pound slab bacon

4 leeks, white part only, trimmed and thinly sliced

Kosher salt and freshly ground black pepper

2 tablespoons peanut oil

¾ pound fingerling or other all-purpose potatoes, scrubbed and sliced ⅛ to ¼ inch thick

1 teaspoon unsalted butter

1 tablespoon fresh thyme leaves

2 tablespoons diced black truffle (optional)

1. Cut the bacon into thin strips about 2 inches long. Cook the bacon in a large skillet over medium heat until rendered but not yet crisp, about 2 minutes. Add the leeks, salt, and pepper and cook, stirring frequently, until the leeks begin to soften, about 5 minutes. Transfer the leeks and bacon to a plate.

2. Wipe out the skillet. Add the oil and heat over medium heat until it slides easily across the pan. Add the potatoes, butter, salt, and pepper and cook until the potatoes are golden, about 3 minutes per side. Add the thyme and the leek mixture and continue cooking, stirring frequently, until the vegetables are tender, about 5 minutes more. If using the truffle, stir it in and serve.

diced potato—leek soup

SERVES 4

4 leeks, white part only, trimmed
¼ pound slab bacon
4 Idaho or other starchy potatoes (3 to
    4 pounds), peeled
1 tablespoon extra-virgin olive oil
Kosher salt and freshly ground black
    pepper

3 cups White Chicken Stock (page 69),
    warmed
2 tablespoons unsalted butter
2 tablespoons chopped fresh chives

1. Split the leeks lengthwise, then slice into thin semicircles. Cut the bacon and potatoes into a small dice.

2. Heat the oil in a large saucepan over medium heat until it slides easily across the pan. Add the bacon and cook until it is rendered but not yet crisp, about 2 minutes. Add the leeks, salt, and pepper and cook, stirring frequently, until the leeks just begin to soften, about 3 minutes. Reduce the heat to medium-low and add the potatoes. Cook, stirring frequently, until the potatoes soften slightly, 3 to 5 minutes more.

3. Add enough stock to moisten the vegetables, about ½ cup. Bring the soup to a simmer, then add another ½ cup of stock. Continue gradually adding the stock, ½ cup at a time, until it has all been added. Gently simmer the soup until the potatoes are tender (about 10 minutes from the time you begin adding stock), then stir in the butter and chives. Add salt and pepper and serve immediately.

roasted potatoes, leeks, and bacon

SERVES 4

I call for slab bacon in this recipe, since sliced bacon will give you too small a dice to "feel" in your mouth alongside the potatoes and leeks. Slab bacon—available at specialty groceries and butchers—tends to be of a higher quality as well.

3 leeks, white part only, trimmed
2 Yukon gold or other all-purpose potatoes, scrubbed
¼ pound slab bacon

2 tablespoons extra-virgin olive oil
Kosher salt and freshly ground black pepper
2 sprigs of fresh thyme

1. Heat the oven to 350° F. Quarter the leeks lengthwise. Slice the potatoes and dice the bacon. Heat the oil in a large ovenproof skillet over medium-high until it shimmers. Add the leeks, potatoes, bacon, salt, pepper, and thyme. Cook, turning the vegetables frequently, until the leeks and potatoes begin to brown.

2. Transfer the skillet to the oven and roast the vegetables, turning occasionally, until they are tender, about 15 minutes. Serve warm.

Over the past few years, green-markets have started to offer "heirloom" potatoes in a host of sizes and dusty colors, from purplish blue to bright yellow and white. I use all types in my cooking: corollas, yellow Finns, Ratte, ruby crescents. Experiment with different varieties to find the texture and flavors you like best.

boulangerie potatoes

In small French villages, there used to be one central bakery, or *boulangerie*. After the daily bread had been baked, the villagers would use the oven to roast food for the evening meal. Meats were roasted on a rack high in the oven, and the potatoes were roasted beneath them, to catch the drippings from above. Using bacon, stock, and leeks helps create the *boulangerie* effect.

¼ pound slab bacon
4 medium leeks, white part only, trimmed
Kosher salt and freshly ground black pepper
2 tablespoons fresh thyme leaves

1¾ pounds Idaho or other starchy potatoes, peeled
1 cup Brown Chicken Stock (page 70), warm
2 tablespoons unsalted butter

1. Heat the oven to 325°F. Cut the bacon into thin strips about 2 inches long. Cut the leeks in half lengthwise, then slice them into thin semicircles. Cook the bacon over medium heat in a large skillet until rendered but not yet crisp, about 2 minutes. Add the leeks, salt, and pepper and cook, stirring frequently, until the leeks begin to soften, about 5 minutes. Add half the thyme leaves and cook, stirring frequently, until the leeks are tender, about 5 minutes more.

> Choose older, starchy potatoes for this dish. They will hold together better than very young or waxy varieties. Don't rinse them, either; the starch is essential for the recipe.

2. Cover the bottom of a medium baking dish with the leek mixture. Slice the potatoes very thin. Arrange them, slightly overlapping, in rows over the leeks. Pour the stock evenly over the potatoes, then dot them with butter and sprinkle with salt and pepper and the remaining thyme. Cover the pan tightly with aluminum foil and bake for 1 hour. Remove the foil and continue baking until the potatoes are tender and the edges are beginning to crisp, about 45 minutes more. Serve warm.

brussels sprouts with bacon

Cooking Brussels sprouts whole invariably leads to soft brownish outer leaves and an undercooked center. Separating the leaves from the core and cooking them "loose" is the best way around this problem, plus it gives an unusual presentation to the dish.

10 ounces Brussels sprouts
Kosher salt
¼ pound slab bacon, diced

1 tablespoon fresh thyme leaves
Freshly ground black pepper

1. Remove any torn or discolored outer leaves from the Brussels sprouts. Trim the bases and cut out and discard the cores. Plunge the trimmed Brussels sprouts into boiling salted water and blanch just until the leaves begin to open slightly, 3 to 5 minutes. Rinse under cold water and separate the leaves.

I like to serve Brussels sprouts with a small amount of Apple Cider Sauce, page 79. Add about ½ to ¾ cup of sauce to the pan in the final step, heat through, and serve.

2. Cook the leaves in boiling salted water until tender, 3 to 5 minutes. Rinse under cold water, then blot dry.

3. Cook the bacon over medium heat in a medium pan until rendered but not yet crisp, about 5 minutes. Reduce the heat to medium-low and add the Brussels sprouts leaves, thyme, salt, and pepper. Mix gently and serve.

Opposite: Pan-roasted cod, Brussels Sprouts with Bacon, Apple Cider Sauce (recipe, page 79), and Boulangerie Potatoes (recipe, page 244).

a few favorites

a s I worked on this book, I discovered I had a few dishes that can only be called "favorites" for lack of a more specific term. These are recipes I prepare over and over, for a variety of uses, and they run the gamut from the humble and homey—like lentils—to the exalted, like foie gras. I've included them as a final note to the book, since the recipes don't conform to my usual seasonal creative process. Rather, they transcend season and work almost any time, either as accompaniments to other dishes or alone on the plate.

lentils

Lentils are not a "gourmet" food, and yet I use them throughout the year, whenever I'm looking to add an earthy quality to a dish. They lend a comforting bass note to the plate, especially alongside roasted meats and fish. Always try to buy green French lentils, which are more flavorful and hold their shape better than the brown or red varieties.

1½ cups green lentils
1 tablespoon peanut oil
1 onion, peeled and coarsely chopped
1 carrot, peeled and coarsely chopped
1 celery stalk, coarsely chopped
1 leek, white part only, trimmed and
   coarsely chopped

1 garlic clove, peeled and minced
Kosher salt
About 1½ cups White Chicken Stock
   (page 69)

1. Rinse the lentils thoroughly, discarding any stones you find.

2. Heat the oil in a medium saucepan over medium heat until it slides easily across the pan. Add the onion, carrot, celery, leek, garlic, and salt, and cook, stirring occasionally, until the vegetables soften, about 15 minutes. Add the lentils and enough of the stock to cover (about 1 cup) and bring to a simmer. Reduce the heat to medium-low and gently simmer until the stock no longer covers the lentils, about 30 minutes. Add salt and enough of the stock so the lentils are once again covered (about ½ cup). Continue cooking, adding stock if necessary, until the lentils are tender, about 30 minutes more. Discard the aromatic vegetables and serve warm or at room temperature.

foie gras terrine

MAKES 1 MEDIUM (OR 2 SMALL) TERRINE(S)

Foie gras is so inherently lush and decadent—that the less you do to it, the better. The terrine takes about two days from start to finish, mostly due to the extended chilling time, so plan ahead. You can set this entire terrine out for guests with slices of toast, or lay individual slices (about ¾ inch thick) on a plate and garnish with Rhubarb Chutney (page 197) or high-quality aged balsamic vinegar.

1 grade-A foie gras (about 1½ pounds)
1½ teaspoons kosher salt
⅛ teaspoon sugar

¼ teaspoon freshly ground black pepper
½ teaspoon Armagnac or brandy

1. Allow the foie gras to come to room temperature. Carefully pull the two lobes apart. Using a small sharp knife, remove the outer membrane and cut away any green portions and any obvious fat. Working on the smaller lobe first, find the large central vein that joined the two lobes. Carefully lift out the vein and its tributaries with the knife, then remove any blood spots. Set the cleaned lobe aside and repeat, removing the veins and blood spots from the second lobe.

2. Combine the salt, sugar, and pepper. Spread half the salt mixture on a plate, place the foie gras on top, cover with the remaining salt mixture, and sprinkle with the Armagnac or brandy. Wrap the foie gras with plastic wrap and refrigerate for 24 hours.

3. Heat the oven to 250°F. Place the foie gras in an ovenproof skillet or small roasting pan and cook until it is soft throughout and appears slick and shiny (begin checking after about 5 minutes).

4. Remove the foie gras from the oven and fit it into a medium terrine mold or loaf pan (smaller terrines can be made in individual ramekins). Cover the foie with plastic wrap, then using a heavy weight (you will need something that weighs at least 3 pounds—cans work well), press any excess fat out of the foie. Refrigerate the weighted terrine(s) for 24 hours. Unmold, slice, and serve slightly chilled.

HOW TO BUY FOIE GRAS

Foie gras comes in three grades: A, B, and C. I recommend you buy "A" livers, as I do in my restaurants, for their larger size and fewer blemishes. If you are buying foie gras in a store, look for large lobes of a creamy, beige color, without any red bruises—a sure sign of mishandling. For these recipes, "cleaning" the foie gras of as many veins and blood spots as possible is more important than keeping the liver perfectly intact.

poached foie gras

This recipe gives you a similar result to foie gras terrine; however, less fat is lost in poaching, so the result is richer, more luxuriant. Like the terrine, it takes about two days to prepare, so plan ahead. Poached foie gras makes a wonderful cold appetizer, and the leftover stock—subtly imbued with foie gras flavor—can be frozen and used later in place of standard brown chicken stock.

1 grade-A foie gras (about 1½ pounds)
1½ teaspoons kosher salt
⅛ teaspoon sugar
¼ teaspoon freshly ground black pepper

½ teaspoon Armagnac or brandy
About 8 cups Brown Chicken Stock
 (page 70)

1. Allow the foie gras to come to room temperature. Carefully pull the two lobes apart. Using a small sharp knife, remove the outer membrane and cut away any green portions and any obvious fat. Working on the smaller lobe first, find the large central vein that joined the two lobes. Carefully lift out the vein and its tributaries with the knife, then remove any blood spots. Set the cleaned lobe aside and repeat, removing the veins and blood spots from the second lobe.

2. Combine the salt, sugar, and pepper. Spread half the salt mixture on a plate, place the foie gras on top, cover with the remaining salt mixture, and sprinkle with the Armagnac or brandy. Wrap the foie gras with plastic wrap and refrigerate for 24 hours.

3. Roll the foie gras in a clean white dish towel, a napkin, or a triple layer of superfine cheesecloth, forming a tight cylinder 1 to 2 inches thick. Twist the ends as tightly as possible. Tie each end with kitchen string, then twist a little tighter and retie. Repeat with the remaining foie gras, rolling, molding, and tying it into a second cylinder. Chill again for at least 2 hours.

Poached Foie Gras and Foie Gras Terrine.

4. Bring the stock to a simmer in a deep skillet or pot wide enough to hold the wrapped foie gras over medium heat. Reduce the heat to medium-low (the stock should just occasionally bubble) and add the first "sausage," cooking it for 1 minute for each inch of diameter. Remove the cooked foie from the stock and add the second "sausage," also cooking it 1 minute for each inch of diameter.

5. Allow the foie gras to cool for about 15 minutes, then remold the "sausages," twisting, tightening, and forcing the foie gras to expel as much fat as possible. Tie the ends together as tightly as possible with additional string at about 1-inch intervals, then chill for 24 hours. Unwrap, slice, and serve slightly chilled.

pan-fried oysters

This is one of the most delicious ways I know to serve oysters. They take only minutes to prepare, and are impossible to pass up. Larger varieties, like Glidden Point or Belon, work especially well in this recipe. They can be served alone, or as a garnish for chowder.

12 large, fresh oysters
1½ cups flour
Kosher salt and freshly ground black
    pepper

Peanut oil
Lemon wedges

1. Open the oysters and remove them from the shells. Dry the oysters thoroughly with paper towels. Season the flour with salt and pepper, then dredge the oysters in the flour, gently shaking off any excess.

2. Heat about ½ inch of the oil in a small heavy skillet over medium-high heat until it shimmers. Fry the oysters in batches, until they are crisp, 1 to 2 minutes per side. Drain on paper towels, then sprinkle with salt and serve with the lemon wedges.

After being harvested, live oysters continue to open and shut. Occasionally, an oyster that has been shipped on its side loses its juices when it opens, causing it to shrivel and die. To avoid buying a "bad" oyster, choose those that are closed and feel heavy for their size. Go ahead and bang them together; steer clear of the ones that sound hollow.

cured salmon

SERVES 8 AS AN APPETIZER, OR 4 AS A MAIN COURSE

Cured salmon is a dish that fits easily into any season, depending on your choice of garnish. I like to serve it sliced paper thin, drizzled with extra-virgin olive oil and fresh herbs. It also works nicely garnished with Marinated Mushrooms (page 113) or alongside a small fennel salad, for lunch.

1½ cups coarsely chopped mixed fresh
    herbs (such as dill, tarragon, parsley,
    chervil, and scallion tops)
1 cup kosher salt
⅓ cup sugar

Zest of 1 lime, finely chopped
Zest of 1 orange, finely chopped
Zest of 1 lemon, finely chopped
1½ pounds salmon fillet

1. Combine the herbs, salt, and sugar in a medium bowl, then add the lime, orange, and lemon zest and mix well.

2. Lay a large piece of plastic wrap on a plate. Use about half of the herb mixture to make a bed for the salmon in the center of the plastic. Place the salmon on top, skin-side down, then cover with the remaining herb mixture. Wrap the salmon tightly in the plastic and refrigerate for 36 hours.

3. Unwrap the salmon and brush off and discard the herb mixture. Blot off any excess moisture with paper towels, then dry the salmon, uncovered, on a plate in the refrigerator for about 1 hour. Slice thin on the bias and serve.

When buying salmon, look for a firm fillet that is intact, without any bruises or tears. If you can find it, I recommend wild salmon, which is more flavorful than the widely available farmed variety. (See Resources, page 264, for sourcing suggestions.)

lemon confit

I love the way curing lemons makes them less aggressive and turns the fruit into a savory ingredient. Preserved lemons are a Middle Eastern dish, with quartered lemons traditionally preserved in a mixture of salt, sugar, black sesame seeds, and saffron. My take on this classic condiment calls for thinly sliced lemons, flavored with garlic and shallots. I use lemon confit over and over again in my cooking— usually alongside roasted chicken or fish. It also works nicely chopped and puréed into a vinaigrette.

12 lemons	⅔ cup kosher salt
5 shallots, peeled and minced	⅓ cup sugar
6 garlic cloves, peeled and minced	Extra-virgin olive oil

1. Plunge the lemons into boiling water (this softens the outer layer of wax). Drain, rinse, then wipe the lemons clean. Dry the lemons, then slice them very thin. Discard the ends and remove and discard the seeds.

2. Combine the shallots with the garlic. Mix the salt with the sugar. Arrange a layer of lemon slices in the bottom of a midsized container with a lid. Sprinkle the lemons first with a little of the shallot mixture, then with some of the salt mixture. Repeat, layering lemons and sprinkling them with the shallot and salt mixtures until the final lemon slices are topped with the last of the salt and shallot mixtures. Cover the container and refrigerate the confit for 3 days. The confit can be used immediately or covered with olive oil and stored in the refrigerator for about a month.

cannellini beans

I use this bean recipe often, adding the cannellinis to the final stage of a braise, as I do in the Braised Lamb Shanks with Roasted Tomato (page 104), or purée-ing them into a flavorful, hearty soup. Always remember to start beans in cold water and cook them slowly on the lowest setting possible on your stove. If you can't find cannellini beans, any dried white bean will do.

2 cups cannellini or other small, dried white beans
1 onion, peeled and quartered
1 carrot, peeled and halved
1 celery rib
1 sprig of fresh tarragon
1 sprig of fresh thyme
Kosher salt and freshly ground black pepper

1. Rinse and pick over the beans and place them in a large pot. Add the onion, carrot, celery, tarragon, thyme, salt, and pepper and enough water to cover by 3 inches (about 8 cups). Bring the beans to a simmer over medium heat. Reduce the heat to medium-low and cook very slowly, stirring occasionally, until the beans are tender. (Begin checking after about 45 minutes.)

2. Remove the beans from the heat and allow them to cool in the cooking liquid. Discard the aromatic vegetables and herbs. Use the beans immediately or store in the cooking liquid in the refrigerator for 3 to 5 days.

my favorite chicken soup

Sunday nights usually find me at home, with remote control in hand—especially during basketball season. This soup is my favorite meal to enjoy in that relaxed mode. Since I know there are as many recipes for chicken soup as there are grand-mothers in the world, I do not offer this as *the* definitive recipe; only as my personal favorite. In deference to my grandmother, I serve it as she did, finished with a dash of olive oil and a grating of Parmigiano over the bowl.

1 chicken, quartered, with bones intact (i.e., do not remove breast meat from breastbone), including necks and giblets
2 carrots, peeled and cut in half
2 celery stalks, washed and cut in half
2 leeks, washed and sliced in half
2 parsnips, peeled and cut in half
1 onion, peeled and cut in half

1 sprig of fresh thyme
Kosher salt and freshly ground black pepper
1½ cups small shell pasta (optional)
Freshly grated Parmigiano-Reggiano (optional)
Extra-virgin olive oil (optional)
Coarse sea salt

1. Place 1 gallon water and the chicken in a stockpot and bring to a simmer over medium heat. Simmer gently, skimming regularly, until the broth is fragrant, for about 30 minutes.

Simmering the soup gently keeps the chicken from shredding apart.

2. Add the vegetables and thyme and continue to simmer for another 20 minutes. Season with salt and pepper.

3. Bring a large pot of salted water to a boil over high heat. Add the pasta and cook until tender, about 8 minutes. Drain, and divide the cooked pasta among 4 bowls.

4. Remove the chicken with a slotted spoon and place on a serving dish. Ladle the broth and vegetables over the pasta and serve with grated Parmigiano (if using), more freshly ground pepper, and a splash of extra-virgin olive oil if desired. Sprinkle the chicken with coarse sea salt and serve alongside the soup.

resources

INGREDIENTS

There is a dizzying array of superior products on the market today, and just as many inferior versions (attractive packaging usually tells you little about the quality of what's inside). Here I've included a few suggestions for detecting the difference.

olive oils and vinegars

There is a great range of quality in olive oils and vinegars, reflecting the difference between small, artisanal producers and the mass-produced varieties. Where possible, buy the best you can afford, not as status items, but because they will add pronounced depth and flavor to your cooking. With the best extra-virgin olive oils and vinegars, you will need only a small amount for an optimal result.

Fine olive oil can have a clean, buttery flavor, or grassy "green" notes. Some are fruity and almost sweet, while others have a peppery bite. What all fine olive oils share are a liveliness of flavor (I prefer other oils—like peanut—when I need a neutral flavor) and a freshness that you can smell as well as taste.

When buying vinegar, look for aged wine vinegars and genuine balsamic vinegar from Modena, Italy. Good balsamic vinegar will have a syrupy viscosity and a balance of acid and sweetness. Steer clear of anything labeled "balsamic condiment," which is not the genuine article.

Always buy extra-virgin olive oils and vinegars in smaller bottles, as they lose freshness soon after opening.

coarse sea salt

Many of my recipes call for a final sprinkling of coarse sea salt, which has a vibrant, nonchemical flavor that I like. Sea salt is harvested off the coast of France, where pristine seawater is drawn into traps, and then left in the sun to evaporate, leaving the salt behind in large crystals. The top layer, known as *Fleur de Sel,* is bleached by the sun and has a clean, white appearance. *Sel Gris,* harvested just below the top layer, is moister and gray in color. Both varieties can be used interchangeably and are available in specialty food stores as well as from the following purveyor:

Marché aux Delices
tel.: 888-547-5471; 212-860-4927
Web site: www.auxdelices.com
E-mail: staff@auxdelices.com

For use during cooking, I recommend a good, basic kosher salt like Diamond Crystal, available in most supermarkets.

The following sources will ship ingredients directly to you and are my preferred purveyors for the ingredients I use.

duck, duck fat, squab, chicken, rabbit, and game bird

D'Artagnan
tel.: 800-DARTAGN (800-327-8246), ext. 118
fax: 973-465-1870
Web site: www.dartagnan.com
E-mail: Tina@dartagnan.com

fresh fish, shellfish, and lobsters

I recommend you find a great fish market in your area, easily accomplished by talking to your favorite chef and asking which retail outlets he or she recommends. It is worthwhile to establish a relationship with the owner so that he or she can steer you to the freshest fish in the store.

As a rule, it is better to buy whole fish rather than fillets although obviously—unless you are cooking for a crowd—this is not always possible. Look for bright, red gills and clear, unclouded eyes, which indicate freshness. The scales should be intact and the flesh should feel firm, not soggy or spongy (a sign of age). Do not assume that everything in the market is of equal and optimal freshness. Ask when the fish arrived and touch before buying.

Browne Trading Company, Inc.
tel.: 800-944-7848; 207-766-2402
fax: 207-766-2404
Web site: www.browne-trading.com
E-mail: markgrobman@browne-trading.com

Wild Edibles
Market at Grand Central Station
42nd Street and Lexington Avenue
tel.: 212-687-4255
fax: 212-687-4477

meats

You'll notice that many of my recipes call for a specific thickness or cut of meat, which will affect the cooking time and the final results of the dish. For this reason, I advise you to form a relationship with a good butcher in your area. In most cases, he or she will be happy to cut meat to your specifications.

Try to buy either prime or choice grades of meat. Prime is hard to come by (what little there is is usually allocated for restaurants) but choice is still good. Look for dry-aged steaks, which have less water, higher fat, and, hence, more flavor.

Piccinini Brothers
tel.: 212-581-7731

In most cases, when cooking, you can substitute different vegetables or meat ingredients in a recipe, based on your own preference or what is readily available. There are some specialty ingredients, however, for which there are simply no substitutes, like foie gras or truffles. Although these ingredients are expensive, I would urge you to splurge on them for special occasions, rather than attempt to substitute a more economical ingredient in their place.

wild mushrooms and truffles

For advice on selecting wild mushrooms, see page 109.

Urbani Truffles USA
tel.: 800-281-2330; 718-392-5050
fax: 718-391-1704
Web site: www.urbani.com
E-mail: urbaniusa@aol.com

Marché aux Delices
tel.: 888-547-5471; 212-860-4927
Web site: www.auxdelices.com
E-mail: staff@auxdelices.com

foie gras

D'Artagnan
tel.: 800-DARTAGN (800-327-8246), ext. 118
fax: 973-465-1870
Web site: www.dartagnan.com
E-mail: Tina@dartagnan.com

specialty produce, such as ramps and white asparagus

Marché aux Delices
tel.: 888-547-5471; 212-860-4927
Web site: www.auxdelices.com
E-mail: staff@auxdelices.com

caviar

Browne Trading Company, Inc.
tel.: 800-944-7848; 207-766-2402
fax: 207-766-2404
Web site: www.browne-trading.com
E-mail: markgrobman@browne-trading.com

EQUIPMENT

Here are the tools that I used in preparing the recipes in this book, along with a few purchasing suggestions.

knives and slicing equipment

10-inch chef knife (I like Wusthof best)
10-inch slicing knife
4-inch paring knife
Sharpening steel
Mandoline (I recommend the inexpensive Japanese variety, which also works for slicing truffles)

pots and saucepans

The pricier brands usually have a layer of conductive metal that wraps partly up the sides to protect food from burning, making them a better value. I recommend buying the best quality you can afford, either heavy-bottomed stainless steel or copper, in the following sizes, which will accommodate all of the recipes in this book:

6-inch sauté pan
10-inch sauté pan
12-inch sauté pan
12-quart stockpot
1-quart straight-sided saucepan
2-quart straight-sided saucepan
Roasting pan

acknowledgments

Writing a book, like cooking a great meal, is a collaborative thing; even the most solitary chef understands the importance of the farmers, artisans, and teachers without whom he or she could never begin. Writing a book is the same. Without many of the people who follow I might never have started, and certainly would not have finished this book.

First and foremost, I would like to thank my mother, Beverly Colicchio, who taught me early that food expresses love, and my father, Tom, who was never far from my thoughts during the writing of this book. Thank you to all the members of my family, who offered reminders of our colorful shared history and who have supported me in each of my endeavors. Thank you especially to my son, Dante, for understanding when Dad gets busy and for helping me to see things through a child's magic eyes.

There are too many talented and helpful people at Gramercy Tavern to thank individually. Together, they kept the restaurant running like a well-oiled machine, freeing me to concentrate on this book. I'd like to thank my entire kitchen staff, especially to John Shaefer, who shows up early every day so I don't have to. Thank you to Modesto Batista for his top-flight delivery system; there were many mornings when the progress of this book depended entirely upon his arrival. I'd like to acknowledge Stacy Lott for her help, her warmth, and her computer skills. Thank you also to my partners, Danny Meyer and Robert Scott.

Many people gave or lent generously of their products to help the book come about. Thank you to Evan Cole and Jeffrey Fazio of ABC Carpet and Home and Dominique Melee of Bernadaud for their beautiful platters, props, and cookware. Many thanks to George Faisan of D'Artagnan, Thierry Farges of Marché aux Delices, and John Jobaggy, who were all generous with their fine ingredients.

Thank you to the entire team at Clarkson Potter, especially my editor, Roy Finamore, for giving us plenty of rope (but not enough to hang ourselves), and Marysarah Quinn, for her beautiful design. Thank you to my agent, Susan Lescher, and to Bill Bettencourt, whose shots of me, a few tomatoes, and my squirming four-year-old years ago led me to deduce he'd make a first-class cookbook photographer (I was right). Without question, I owe thanks to Sean Fri, who bugged me to write a book in the first place and whose brainy, idiosyncratic approach to life helped me envision something other than just a book full of recipes.

The people who know me well know that my idea of hell is writing down a recipe. I owe enormous gratitude to my friend and colleague Cathy Young, who shouldered the task of translating my fists of herbs into something quantifiable. She did more than just test the recipes; she gave of herself. Lastly, thanks to Lori Silverbush, who somehow filled the pages of this book with my voice and my heart with love.

Tom Colicchio

index

Note: Boldfaced page references indicate sidebars. Italicized page references indicate photographs.

conversion chart
equivalent imperial and metric measurements

American cooks use standard containers, the 8-ounce cup and a tablespoon that takes exactly 16 level fillings to fill that cup level. Measuring by cup makes it very difficult to give weight equivalents, as a cup of densely packed butter will weigh considerably more than a cup of flour. The easiest way therefore to deal with cup measurements in recipes is to take the amount by volume rather than by weight. Thus the equation reads:

1 cup = 240 ml = 8 fl. oz.   ½ cup = 120 ml = 4 fl. oz.

It is possible to buy a set of American cup measures in major stores around the world.

In the States, butter is often measured in sticks. One stick is the equivalent of 8 tablespoons (½ cup). One tablespoon of butter is therefore the equivalent to ½ ounce/15 grams.

liquid measures

Fluid Ounces	U.S.	Imperial	Milliliters
	1 teaspoon	1 teaspoon	5
¼	2 teaspoons	1 dessertspoon	10
½	1 tablespoon	1 tablespoon	14
1	2 tablespoons	2 tablespoons	28
2	¼ cup	4 tablespoons	56
4	½ cup		110
5		¼ pint or 1 gill	140
6	¾ cup		170
8	1 cup		225
9			250, ¼ liter
10	1¼ cups	½ pint	280
12	1½ cups		340
15		¾ pint	420
16	2 cups		450
18	2¼ cups		500, ½ liter
20	2½ cups	1 pint	560
24	3 cups		675
25		1¼ pints	700
27	3½ cups		750
30	3¾ cups	1½ pints	840
32	4 cups or 1 quart		900
35		1¾ pints	980
36	4½ cups		1000, 1 liter
40	5 cups	2 pints or 1 quart	1120

solid measures

U.S. and Imperial Measures		Metric Measures	
Ounces	Pounds	Grams	Kilos
1		28	
2		56	
3½		100	
4	¼	112	
5		140	
6		168	
8	½	225	
9		250	¼
12	¾	340	
16	1	450	
18		500	½
20	1¼	560	
24	1½	675	
27		750	¾
28	1¾	780	
32	2	900	
36	2¼	1000	1
40	2½	1100	
48	3	1350	
54		1500	1½

oven temperature equivalents

Fahrenheit	Celsius	Gas Mark	Description
225	110	¼	Cool
250	130	½	
275	140	1	Very Slow
300	150	2	
325	170	3	Slow
350	180	4	Moderate
375	190	5	
400	200	6	Moderately Hot
425	220	7	Fairly Hot
450	230	8	Hot
475	240	9	Very Hot
500	250	10	Extremely Hot

Any broiling recipes can be used with the grill of the oven, but beware of high-temperature grills.

equivalents for ingredients

all-purpose flour—plain flour
coarse salt—kitchen salt
cornstarch—cornflour
eggplant—aubergine

half and half—12% fat milk
heavy cream—double cream
light cream—single cream
lima beans—broad beans

scallion—spring onion
unbleached flour—strong, white flour
zest—rind
zucchini—courgettes or marrow